Decision analysis

R G Coyle
University of Bradford

Decision analysis

Nelson

Thomas Nelson and Sons Ltd
36 Park Street London WIY 4DE

PO Box 18123 Nairobi Kenya

Thomas Nelson (Australia) Ltd
597 Little Collins Street Melbourne 3000

Thomas Nelson and Sons (Canada) Ltd
81 Curlew Drive Don Mills Ontario

Thomas Nelson (Nigeria) Ltd
PO Box 336 Apapa Lagos

Thomas Nelson and Sons (South Africa) (Proprietary) Ltd
51 Commissioner Street Johannesburg

First published in Great Britain 1972
Copyright © R G Coyle 1972
0 17 761017 4 (boards)
0 17 771017 9 (paper)

Printed in Great Britain by
The Camelot Press Ltd, London and Southampton

Contents

Preface

This book aims to introduce practising managers and management students to the more useful and interesting parts of decision theory. It does this in such a way as to bring out the significance of the theory to practical problems while avoiding formal mathematical treatment. The only mathematical skill needed to read and understand the book is simple arithmetic coupled with willingness and some effort.

The book is not intended to be a formal exposition of mathematical decision theory but a limited amount of mathematical shorthand is employed. This is carefully explained as it is introduced. There are a couple of simple mathematical appendices but these can be ignored without losing the thread of the argument or failing to grasp the managerial significance of the results of the algebra. The reader who finds himself becoming fogged by arithmetic should skip over it and concentrate on the non-arithmetical parts of the book. In this way he will absorb the essential flavour and managerial significance of the theory. After he has done this he could well reread the parts he has found difficult, paying closer attention to the arithmetic.

The general approach is by example and illustration rather than by mathematical logic. Each topic is introduced by expressing it in terms of a managerial decision problem which is then solved by the methods of decision theory. This treatment is reinforced by problems with fully-worked solutions for the reader who wishes to go a little further with the subject.

In general, the book should be useful for the practising manager either at work or attending a short course, the student working for the Diploma in Management Studies, or for the less mathematically inclined student at the start of a master's degree in a university. For a more advanced treatment the reader may refer to my *Mathematics for Business Decisions*.

As always my wife and children come out on top of the list of people to be thanked publicly. Miss Dianne Dobson patiently coped with the typing of a horribly written manuscript.

R G Coyle

1

Decision making

1.1 Introduction

This book is concerned with methods of analysing decision problems and selecting attractive courses of action. We shall be dealing with some fairly weighty problems and it would be as well to try to establish some clear idea of what is meant by the terms to be used. The best way of doing this is to examine and solve an illustrative decision problem.

1.2 The Hopeless Transport Company

The Hopeless Transport Company operates a small fleet of long-distance haulage vehicles and the time has now come when some of them have to be replaced. There are two vehicle types available—A, which they already use, and B which is cheaper to buy and run but which will be more expensive to maintain if it proves to be less robust in service than A. The B vehicles have only recently been introduced to the market so that the haulage industry has had little chance to evaluate their maintenance needs. The A type has been in service for many years and has a good maintenance record but some batches have been known to need a lot of maintenance. For simplicity, the Hopeless Transport Company categorize the maintenance as low or high and, by a mixture of costing and inspired guesswork, arrive at a table showing the net income, allowing for maintenance, which results from buying A or B and the maintenance being high or low. Expressed in suitable financial units per year (which we shall ignore in order not to cloud the issue) it is:

Hopeless Transport Company net income (pay off) table

		Maintenance needed	
		High	Low
Vehicle bought	A	10	15
	B	8	20

This is called a **pay off** table and the figures are, as we have said, the net incomes from each vehicle type if the maintenance turned out to be low or high.

Before trying to solve the problem we can define some of our terms and examine the problem structure. First of all, the costs in the table are called **conditional outcomes**. Thus, the outcome of 20 will only happen if B has been bought and the maintenance turns out to be low. The result 10 is similarly conditional upon the choice 'buy A' and the result 'maintenance is high'.

This last sentence illustrates two of the essential features of a decision problem—**choice** and **outcome**. If there is no choice available then one has no decision problem and Hobson's choice is no choice at all. If, given a choice, the outcome is known with certainty we have a particular type of decision problem and the problem of deciding which choice to make is rather simpler. Such a problem is called **deterministic** because the outcome is completely fixed or determined once we have made the choice. In the case of the Hopeless Transport Company, the choice of vehicle does not fix the outcome and maintenance costs can still be low or high. This is called a **stochastic** decision problem because the outcome is fixed by random events (such as the way in which the maintenance needed is affected by the state of the manu- facturing methods employed by the supplier of the A vehicles) or at any rate by circumstances about which we know so little that we are forced to treat them as random. The word 'stochastic' derives from the Greek for a target— the allusion being to the uncertainty of hitting it.

If we now pose the question of which choice should the Hopeless Transport Company make, we identify the third component of a decision problem—the **criterion**. We cannot recommend a course of action or choose one for ourselves unless we make up our minds what it is that we wish to do.

In this book we shall examine the use of several criteria, starting with some of the simpler ones.

1.3 The maximin criterion

The Hopeless Transport Company is not in very good financial shape and they feel that, although they have to replace their fleet, they must avoid the worst outcomes if possible. They therefore choose as their criterion the **maximin** rule which is 'choose the action which maximizes the minimum pay off which can be achieved'.

If the Hopeless Transport Company buy type A vehicles then the worst that can happen is that the maintenance will be high and the outcome will be 10. On the other hand, if they choose B then the worst outcome will be 8. Of these two values 10 is larger than 8 so it is the maximum of the minimum pay offs and the Hopeless Transport Company choose to buy the A vehicles.

We can formalize this procedure into two simple rules:

1   Choose the lowest value in each row and write it at the end of the row.
2   Look through these smallest values and find the largest. That row gives the optimal or ideal choice.

Applying the rules to the pay off table we would have:

		Maintenance		*Smallest value in the*	*Optimal*
		High	*Low*	*row*	*choice*
Choice	A	10	15	10	⇐
	B	8	20	8	

1.4 A further example of maximin

Mass Marketing Ltd, has four new products A, B, C, and D of which it can introduce one. The introduction of a product is an action and each of the four actions can have three outcomes—in this case suppose that they are levels of demand for the product. The pay off table has been estimated to be:

		Outcome		
		I	II	III
	A	20	40	30
Action	B	80	70	– 10
	C	90	10	– 20
	D	10	100	40

The maximin procedure applied to this pay off table yields:

		Outcome			*Minimum*	*Optimal*
		I	II	III	*value*	*choice*
	A	20	40	30	20	⇐
Action	B	80	70	– 10	– 10	
	C	90	10	– 20	– 20	
	D	10	100	40	10	

The maximin rule directs us to choose A despite the very large returns which, with favourable outcomes, could be achieved by actions B, C, or D.

The maximin rule is very defensive. It may be the right one to use in some circumstances but it is tantamount to asserting that a bird in the hand is worth *any* number in the bush. Few managers would really be able to justify that statement except in very exceptional circumstances.

1.5 Opportunity loss

The maximin decision rule is clearly unsuitable so we are forced to develop more powerful ways of attacking decision problems.

If, in the last problem, we had chosen action A and it had turned out later that the outcome had been II we should be considerably annoyed. Choosing A has given us a pay off of 40 whereas if we had known in advance that outcome II was going to happen we should have chosen action D and had a pay off of 100. In a very real sense we should have lost the opportunity to make an extra 60 units of pay off. This prompts the idea that we should rephrase the pay off table to show not conditional outcomes but conditional **opportunity losses**. We could then invent a decision rule which would ensure that we missed as few opportunities as possible.

Opportunity losses are calculated quite easily from ordinary pay off tables by:

1 Finding the largest number in the column.

2 Subtracting each entry in the table from the largest number in the appropriate column and writing the answer in place of the original entry.

Applying these rules to the example we have a new table—a conditional opportunity loss table or COL table.

COL table for Mass Marketing Ltd

		Outcome		
		I	II	III
Action	A	70	60	10
	B	10	30	50
	C	0	90	60
	D	80	0	0

We observe the rule that $40-(-20)=60$, i.e., a double negative becomes positive.

Notice now that there are three zeros in the table. These mean that if we had known what the outcome was to be we could have made an optimal choice of action, i.e., one which would not have led to any lost opportunity. This particular example has no zeros in the first row, i.e., action A always leads to lost opportunity even though the maximin criterion identifies it as a nice safe policy.

1.6 The minimax criterion

With the opportunity loss concept we use the criterion of minimizing the maximum opportunity loss. It no longer makes sense to try to use the old decision rule of maximizing the minimum pay off.

The minimax criterion uses the steps:

1 Select the maximum value in each row of the COL table.

2 Choose the action which has the smallest of these maximum values.

Applying these rules to the Mass Marketing Ltd COL table leads to:

		Outcome			Maximum value in row	Optimal action
		I	II	III		
Action	A	70	60	10	70	
	B	10	30	50	50	⇐
	C	0	90	60	90	
	D	80	0	0	80	

The minimax opportunity loss decision criterion bids us select action B, as opposed to action A picked out by the maximin rule. It is quite usual for these two rules to lead to different optimal acts and it is not in the least surprising that this should be the case. The two rules are entirely different and it is therefore to be expected that they will lead to different courses of action.

To summarize
The maximin pay off rule identifies a course of action which guarantees that we avoid the very worst that can befall and leads to a choice based on the least of many evils.

The minimax opportunity loss gives us the action about which there will be the least regret for foregone opportunities. In fact, the term 'regret' is often used in place of 'opportunity loss'. The word 'opportunity' has to be stressed or the untutored manager may reply, rather abruptly, that he is not interested in minimizing his losses. These are not necessarily actual cash losses—they are foregone opportunities.

1.7 Dummy actions
The Hopeless Transport Company has the chance to move into three new areas of business, A, B, or C, in each of which the demand for their services may be, they think, low, medium, or high. Having improved their market research and costing they draw up a pay off table which includes both expenditure and income.

		Market state (outcome)		
		Low	Medium	High
Action	A	− 80	− 40	− 5
	B	− 30	− 20	− 15
	C	− 90	− 10	− 10

Even allowing for revenue they are going to make losses. However, they apply the maximin and the minimax opportunity loss rules to see what they should do. The working looks like:

Maximin pay off

		Outcome			Minimum	Optimal
		L	M	H	pay off	choice
Action	A	− 80	− 40	− 5	− 80	
	B	− 30	− 20	− 15	− 30	⇐
	C	− 90	− 10	− 10	− 90	

Minimax opportunity loss
The pay off table has to be converted into a COL table and the minimax rules can then be applied.

		Outcome			Maximum opportunity	Optimal
		L	M	H	loss	choice
Action	A	50	30	0	50	
	B	0	10	10	10	⇐
	C	60	0	5	60	

This is rather comforting because both rules direct the Hopeless Transport Company to the same action. It may also be fallacious as even action B is not exactly an entertaining profit prospect. The fallacy here is the fact that there is always the choice of doing nothing so there are really four actions, whereas the Hopeless Transport Company has only considered the obvious three. The moral is that no amount of decision analysis, even employing the more sophisticated methods developed later in the book, will lead to profitable action if the problem has not been defined properly in the first place. It is, in fact, a weakness of the opportunity loss table that, from the way it is calculated, it only contains zero or positive entries (if it contains negatives the arithmetic is wrong!). This rather obscures the fact that the pay off table may contain losses. It is sensible to check that the indicated policy really is the one to be followed.

In the case of the Hopeless Transport Company the fourth course, doing nothing, may have one of three outcomes, either there is a zero pay off or there is a large negative pay off corresponding to the case where failing to offer a full range of services could lead to large losses from idle equipment and lost business on other services, or there may be a positive pay off from the sale of surplus equipment.

We can deal with whichever of the three possibilities is appropriate by introducing a fourth row, D, to the pay off table with suitable values in the row. In the first case, these values will all be zero, in the third case they would be positive. In the second case, the values would theoretically be the foregone income or the costs of going out of business. In practice these values are nearly impossible to determine with any pretension of accuracy so we can replace them by numbers which are merely large (and negative) in relation to those already in the pay off table. In this example, the most negative value in the table is -90 so we might put in a D row of -500 say. Another alternative would be to say that the costs of doing nothing are so large that there is no question of doing nothing and the problem then returns to being one with three courses of action.

We can illustrate the calculation by choosing the first case, where there is zero pay off from doing nothing. We observe that zero is larger than a negative number.

The pay off table is now:

| | | Outcome | | |
		L	M	H
	A	-80	-40	-5
Action	B	-30	-20	-15
	C	-90	-10	-10
	D	0	0	0

and the COL table is:

		Outcome		
		L	M	H
	A	80	40	5
Action	B	30	20	15
	C	90	10	10
	D	0	0	0

Using either the maximin pay off or the minimax opportunity loss criterion the optimal act is D— do nothing. Clearly, the two criteria lead to results which are in accordance with common sense when the problem is phrased properly.

In passing, we note that the two decision rules of maximin pay off and minimax opportunity loss have now pointed to the same conclusion whereas in Sections 1.4 and 1.6 they gave conflicting indications for Mass Marketing Ltd. There is no contradiction in this. The two rules are fundamentally different and whether they give the same or contradictory answers depends entirely on the numbers in the problem. In fact, these two problems have been constructed to illustrate examples of conflict and concord in the results.

1.8 Refining the theory

The theory which has been presented so far has one fundamental weakness— it takes no account of the likelihood of different outcomes taking place. It does not even assume that all outcomes are equally likely and the whole idea of expectations is ignored. This is frankly unreasonable except in special circumstances. In most cases, managers would have some kind of estimate, even if it was completely unrealistic, of what might happen. Since this kind of feeling or assumption about likelihood, no matter how imperfectly based on evidence, is bound to influence management's decision-making then our decision theory should take explicit account of it.

For instance, the minimax opportunity loss rule indicates to Mass Marketing Ltd that action B should be taken. Although the Mass Marketing Ltd Management cannot know for certain what the outcome will be, what would happen if all their experience, judgement, and knowledge indicated that outcome III was virtually certain? In this case, they would wish to take action D or perhaps A which is nearly as good. This would still be true even with a very defensive outlook because if III happens after they have chosen B (we are assuming that the decisions are irreversible) then there will be a loss of 10. Notice that if, by contrast, they felt strongly outcome I was going to be the result they could quite happily stick to action B and if outcome II was expected they would not do too badly by staying with action B. In short, expectation is going to have a strong influence on decision making and we must extend our theory of decisions to cover the ideas of expectation or probability and their incorporation into the pay off table.

Problems

1. A decision problem has been expressed in the following pay off table.

		Outcome		
		I	II	III
	A	10	20	25
Action	B	− 30	30	60
	C	40	30	20

What is the maximin pay off action?

2. What is the minimax opportunity loss action for Problem 1?

3. Another decision problem has the pay off table

		Outcome			
		I	II	III	IV
	A	30	40	35	90
	B	60	30	40	30
Action	C	20	15	35	30
	D	40	20	50	60

What are the maximin pay off and minimax opportunity loss actions?

4. The Site Agent for a construction contract has to arrange for the excavation of a large foundation trench. He has no knowledge of what lies below the first few feet of soil but he does know that the area has been used for industry in the past so that he may well find the remains of old walls, pipes, etc. Test drilling would be rather unlikely to find anything as small as a pipe so he has to proceed without any real information. If there are underground obstructions, hiring a small excavator and a large one will be most appropriate, otherwise two large ones should be used. Obviously if there are no underground difficulties and he has hired both a small and large excavator the cost will be greater but it would then be rather too late to change the hiring agreement.

The costs (in £000) would probably be:

	Ground clear	Ground obstructed
One small and one large machine	100	150
Two large machines	80	200

What is the maximin pay off action? Does the optimal strategy change if the Site Agent employs the minimax opportunity loss criterion?

5. Having solved Problem 4 the Site Agent transmits his optimal choice to his Head Office and is briskly told that he hasn't covered enough possibilities and that his estimates are wrong for those possibilities which he has considered. The Chief Engineer says that there are four possible outcomes:

A ground more or less clear;

B ground with wall foundations;

C ground with old drain pipes, etc.;

D ground with walls and pipes.

The Chief Engineer also says that the Site Agent should examine three types of equipment—large excavator, small excavator, and pneumatic demolition equipment. This leaves four conceivable combinations:

  I two large excavators;

 II one large and one small machine;

III I with demolition equipment;

IV II with demolition equipment.

The Chief Engineer (never having seen the site) gives the following estimates:

		Ground state			
		A	B	C	D
Equipment combination	I	70	170	250	270
	II	150	160	200	230
	III	80	140	180	210
	IV	160	120	140	160

The Site Agent contemplates resignation but decides that it really is easier to work the whole problem again.

6. The last problem illustrates a collection of managerial issues which are more important than the arithmetical practice the problem provides. What are they and how would you resolve them?

2

Probability

2.1 The meaning of 'probability'

In the last chapter we said that in order to extend our methods for dealing with decision problems we should like to incorporate ways of analysing expectations about the future and to do this we should need to make use of some probability theory.

This is a very appealing idea because the mathematical theory of probability is highly developed and includes methods for carrying out extensive calculations so that we ought, in principle, to be able to calculate the course of action which is optimal in some sense in a particular set of circumstances. The problem is that the theory of probability is defined by mathematicians in a particular way which does not always coincide with our intuitive notions of the expression 'probable'. We are therefore in danger of relying on a theory which depends on basic assumptions which are not appropriate to the circumstances with which we have to deal, thus running the risk of serious error. This is not to say that probability theory should not be used but merely that we should take some pains to understand the assumptions underlying our actions and check that they are applicable in any particular case.

2.2 Events and probability

An 'event' is a notion used by mathematicians in evolving their theory of probability. An event is simply something which may or may not happen. For instance it may rain or it may not, the maintenance cost may be high or low, the market may grow or flop, and so on. Each of the occurrences 'it rains', 'maintenance cost high', and 'market grows' would be called an **event**. Usually, to economize on space and effort we use letters to stand for events, e.g., let A be the event 'it rains'.

As we have said, it may rain or it may not and if it does we say that A has occurred. In practice it is usually necessary to allow for what happens if A does not occur since the whole point of probability theory is to cope with situations in which events *might* happen rather than those in which events are certain to happen. Thus, if we are talking about the weather we really ought to allow for two events:

A 'it rains';
B 'it does not rain'.

Note that event B includes snow, hail, and hurricane, in fact any other kind of weather which does not involve rain.

Now clearly in any given day either it rains or it does not so that either A or B must happen. Events of which one or other must happen are called **complementary events**. It will be evident that in practice there will be many occasions when we have to allow for more than two complementary events but for the moment we shall stick to the simple case.

Having introduced 'events' we can easily introduce probability by saying that it is our 'expectation', arrived at in some suitable way, that an event will take place. This is expressed by saying that if we are sure an event is going to happen, then its probability will be 1·00. If it is certain not to happen then its probability will be 0·00. If we think that an event may happen then the probability will be somewhere between 0·00 and 1·00. The nearer it is to 1·00 the higher our expectation that it will happen and the nearer it is to 0·00 the lower the expectation. No magic attaches to 0·00 and 1·00 and we often use 0 and 100 and refer to percentages, e.g., 100% probability is certainty.

There is nothing new in the idea of probability or in the use of numbers to express it. Bookmakers and gamblers have used it for centuries. The contribution of mathematics has been to develop methods for finding probabilities and for drawing tenable conclusions from them. Unfortunately, the methods for finding probabilities work rather imperfectly in horse-racing; however, they are far more satisfactory in business. There is no essential difference between gambling and some aspects of business because success in both depends on a correct assessment of the odds. The value of decision theory in business is to ensure that the correct conclusions are drawn from the assessment of probabilities. This is an assertion which the reader must establish for himself by reading this book.

2.3 Basic notions in probability theory

We write the statement that, for example, 'the probability that it will rain is 0·75' as

$$P(A) = 0·75$$

The letter P stands for 'the probability of' and the event to which the probability statement refers is written in brackets.

This, the simplest form of probability, is **unconditional probability**—often referred to as a **simple probability**. As the name implies this is the probability of an event without regard to any other events. For example, if there are two events, A, 'it will rain today' and B, 'it will snow today' and the occurrence of B is quite independent of A and vice-versa, in the sense that raining does not cause snowing and it can snow without it having rained, then one can speak of unconditional probabilities as being $P(A)$ and $P(B)$ respectively.

The essence of probability theory lies in the idea of complementary events which was mentioned earlier. In the first example we had the events, 'A—it rains' and 'B—it does not rain' and we said that A *or* B must happen. We also said that the probability of something which must happen is 1·00. This means that we can think of another event, X, which is 'it rains or it does not rain' and, fairly obviously in this case,

$$P(X) = 1 \cdot 00$$

Now, the event X is really the net result of A *or* B and we denote this by writing

$$X = A \cup B$$

The symbol $\cup$ is short hand for *or* so we now have

$$P(X) = P(A \cup B) = 1 \cdot 00$$

Now, we have just said that either A or B must occur so their total probabilities must add to $1 \cdot 00$. Thus, in this case

$$P(A \cup B) = P(A) + P(B) = 1 \cdot 00$$

We can make this even clearer by calling B 'not A' and denoting it by $\tilde{A}$. As either A or 'not A' has to be the case we have, as before

$$P(A) + P(\tilde{A}) = 1 \cdot 00$$

Another way of using the formulae is to say that if $P(A) = 0 \cdot 75$ then $P(B)$ or $P(\tilde{A})$ has to be $0 \cdot 25$.

The idea of complementarity can be extended to more than two events providing they are **collectively exhaustive and mutually exclusive**. This means that between them they have to cover all possibilities and the occurrence of any one of them has to rule out the occurrence of any other. A collection of probabilities relating to a collectively exhaustive and mutually exclusive set of events is called a **probability distribution**. The individual probabilities must add to $1 \cdot 00$. Thus, if there were three collectively exhaustive and mutually exclusive events A, B, and C we would have

$$P(A) + P(B) + P(C) = 1 \cdot 00$$

We now have the germ of the idea of compound events which we can easily develop.

Suppose we have a set of three collectively exhaustive and mutually exclusive events A, B, and C. Then, as we have seen

$$P(A) + P(B) + P(C) = 1 \cdot 00$$

Now, what is the probability that either, say, A *or* B will occur? Notice from their definition however, they cannot *both* take place. The answer is

$$P(A \cup B) = P(A) + P(B) \tag{2.1}$$

where $A \cup B$ means the **compound event** 'A or B happens'.

2.4 Conditional probability

Usually events do not happen in isolation but are dependent on other events. Thus if the event A is 'a component is faulty' and B is 'the material supplied had defects' then A might very well depend on B and we could say that A was conditional on B.

Suppose we have three events A, B, and C with probabilities

$$P(A)=0\cdot2, \qquad P(B)=0\cdot4, \quad \text{and} \quad P(C)=0\cdot2$$

then

$$P(A\cup B)=P(A)+P(B)=0\cdot2+0\cdot4=0\cdot6$$

Suppose we were told A or B had happened but our informant could not remember which, then what is the probability it was B? Now we know that A or B did happen so, *given that information*, we now need a **conditional probability for B**. This is found by observing that of the original value of 0·6 for $P(A\cup B)$, 0·4 came from $P(B)$ so there is a $0\cdot4/0\cdot6=0\cdot67$ chance it was B that happened because this is the proportion of $P(A\cup B)$ supplied by $P(B)$. This is an example of a probability being dependent on having certain information, or on something else having happened. Conditional probabilities are often written as $P(X|Z)$ which means 'the probability of X given that (the vertical line) Z has happened'.

For instance, suppose it was found in quality control that of those ball bearings which failed to pass a hardness test 60% had surface defects. Then, if A denotes the event 'failed to pass the hardness test' and B is 'had surface defect', $P(B|A)=0\cdot6$.

2.5 Joint probability

Suppose we know that 20% of the ball bearings in the last example will fail the hardness test, what is the probability that a ball bearing will fail the test *and* have surface faults? We are now talking about a **joint event**—in this case 'A happens *and* B happens'—the probability of which we symbolize by $P(A\cap B)$, with $\cap$ meaning 'and'. We know $P(B|A)=0\cdot6$ and $P(A)=0\cdot2$. This says there is a 20% chance that A will take place and, when it has, there is a 60% chance it will be followed by B. Thus 60% of 20% go through A and B so

$$P(A\cap B)=0\cdot20 \times 0\cdot60=0\cdot12$$

In symbols, and generally for any events A and B

$$P(A\cap B)=P(A) \times P(B|A) \tag{2.2}$$

Equation (2.2) is widely used because we can apply to it the ordinary rules of algebraic manipulation to get

$$P(A)=\frac{P(A\cap B)}{P(B|A)} \tag{2.3}$$

and

$$P(B|A)=\frac{P(A\cap B)}{P(A)} \tag{2.4}$$

Equations (2.3) and (2.4) are often used in problems to calculate probabilities which are not otherwise known.

If A and B are independent then we no longer need to use $P(B|A)$ to indicate that B is conditional on A. We simply use $P(B)$ in its own right. The basic form of Eqn (2.3) remains however, and we have

$$P(A \cap B) = P(A) \times P(B) \tag{2.5}$$

Equation (2.5) can be extended to any number of events and the joint probability of them all happening is simply the product of their individual conditional probabilities.

2.6 Overlapping events

It very frequently happens that two events **overlap** in the sense that either or both may take place. For example, if A is the event 'gearbox fails' and B is the event 'transmission snaps' then of course it may very well happen that both A and B occur. This means that A and B are no longer mutually exclusive and the occurrence of one does not rule out the other.

If we had $P(A) = 0.6$ and $P(B) = 0.6$ then we should be tempted to use Eqn (2.1) and put

$$\begin{aligned} P(A \cup B) &= P(A) + P(B) \\ &= 0.6 \quad + 0.6 \quad = 1.2 \end{aligned}$$

Now this contradicts the basic rule which states that a probability can *never* be larger than 1·00. Is the rule at fault or have we overlooked something? Equation (2.1) only applies to mutually exclusive events and in this case A and B are not mutually exclusive. We now have to use the formula

$$P(A \cup B) = P(A) + P(B) - P(A \cap B) \tag{2.6}$$

If we use Eqn (2.1) we shall include, with $P(A)$, those parts of B which overlap with A and, when we add $P(B)$, we shall add these parts of A which overlap with B. These two overlaps are the same so we have double-counted and to avoid this we need to subtract the overlap which is where A and B occur. This is done by including in the formula, $- P(A \cap B)$

As $P(A)$ and $P(B)$ are unconditional probabilities we use the fact from Eqn (2.5)

$$P(A \cap B) = P(A) \times P(B)$$

We now have

$$\begin{aligned} P(A \cup B) &= 0.6 + 0.6 - 0.6 \times 0.6 \\ &= 0.84 \end{aligned}$$

which is more reasonable.

2.7 Probability and repeatability

So far in this chapter we have explained what probability is and we have given some of the more elementary formulae and definitions. (The reader should not attempt to memorize them but should refer to them at need.) We have not yet discussed how we arrive at probabilities and the assumptions which underly the whole idea but have merely said that 'probability' was linked to 'expectation'.

Now, in every day usage we make statements like 'it will probably rain today', 'Damp Squib will probably win the Derby', or 'the shares in the Hopeless Transport Company are probably not worth the paper they are printed on'. In the latter two cases, we may even be prepared to support our statement by backing another horse or buying another company's shares although we know that outsiders sometimes do win races and the holders of unlikely shares occasionally become millionaires.

What then is the link between probability theory and 'probable'? The answer lies in the idea of repeatability. This says that if we agree on what a particular event is to be, for instance a car of a particular make and type having a major breakdown at between 30 000 and 40 000 miles of life, and then observe a suitably large number of cases, counting those in which the event occurs, then the probability of the event is simply the ratio of the number of occurrences to the total number of observations. For instance, if we study 115 cars during this 10 000 mile period, taking due precautions against false readings, and we observe that 74 of them do in fact have a breakdown, i.e., our defined event occurs, then the probability of a breakdown is taken to be $74 \div 115$, i.e., approximately 0·64 or 64% (probabilities are nearly always quoted to two places of decimals). Notice that there is a very important assumption behind this, namely, the information available is based on a particular group of 115 cars. These are by no means all the cars of the same make which have done 30 000 miles and we call it a **sample** of a **population**. All we *know* is that 74 cars out of 115 broke down and we *assume* that the figure of 64% can legitimately be applied to a reasonably large number of similar cars.

If we had information that 74 000 cars out of 115 000 had broken down we should be fairly confident about the assumption. We should be less confident if we knew that 7 out of 11 had broken down, though $75 000 \div 115 000$ and $7 \div 11$ both give the same answer of 0·64 (practically). There is, in fact, a whole body of theory regarding what constitutes a satisfactory sample size and what is a reasonable number to which to apply the sample information, obviously the key word is 'similar'.

Now, the value of 0·64 obtained from the car study means that, on average, we should expect that 64% of all similar cars would have mechanical breakdowns of the type defined. It does not mean that any particular car would have 0·64 of a breakdown. Clearly, this is impossible and a particular car will either fail or it will not. However, we know that in a reasonably long run, about 64% of similar cars can be expected to fail and this is the idea of repeatability. It depends on our assumption that what has been observed to occur will continue to happen.

2.8 Useless Cars Ltd and repeatability

To see how the idea of repeatability will work in a decision problem we consider the case of the Hopeless Transport Company's subsidiary, Useless Cars Ltd. This enterprise has decided to acquire a new fleet of cars to replace its existing 100 taxis. The 'new' cars have, as it happens, just completed

30 000 miles each and Useless Cars Ltd know that the cost of maintenance including a major breakdown will be £100 while the cost of maintenance without one will be £20 during the next 10 000 miles of life. What will be the average cost per car?

Knowing that the breakdown probability based on the information about the sample of 115 cars is taken to be 0·64 and that there are 100 cars means we expect 64 breakdowns and, therefore, 36 ordinary cars. The average cost is thus

$$\frac{64 \times £100 + 36 \times £20}{100} = £71 \cdot 2 \text{ per car}$$

This is a very trivial example of a probability application but it serves to illustrate the way in which, by the presence of fairly large numbers of events, we can use the idea of repeatability to calculate what are called expected values.

It is, therefore, relatively safe to rely on the assumption of repeatability in areas such as quality control, stock control, and so on, and the mathematical formulation of probability and the plain man's idea of 'probable' mesh together rather well. We now examine another case, more typical of decision theory.

2.9 Mass Marketing Ltd and repeatability

Mass Marketing Ltd has just acquired control of Harebrain Ltd—a company which owns the rights in a new air conditioning and central heating unit for houses. This new unit is the size of a small suitcase and works from an ordinary household electrical supply. It is claimed to be totally effective and trouble-free and a unit could be sold for about £4·50 and manufactured for a direct cost of £1·25. Its future should be good and the patentees rich, rather quickly.

The capital costs of setting up production, however, are very high and this is a completely revolutionary product in a new market, so much depends on how large the market becomes. For simplicity, we could categorize the market states as low, medium, and high, with only high being profitable because of the capital costs, but can we apply the idea of repeatability in order to use probability as an aid in decision-making? Suppose, for example, that Dr Harebrain, the inventor, says that he thinks there is a 20% chance of a low market, 20% of a medium market, and 60% of a high market; what exactly does that mean? Apart from what the statement means, has he any basis on which to make it or are they simply numbers conjured from the air? These are serious issues and the unreality of the problem is intended to highlight them. Unless we can answer them we have no real justification for trying to use probability theory.

Taking the probability statement itself first, we know that it should mean that in a reasonably large number of similar cases (perhaps 20 or more) on average about 20% would lead to a low market, 20% to a medium market, and 60% to a high market. However, these products are launched relatively infrequently, and certainly so by any one company, so there is little likelihood of ever having a large number of cases. Furthermore, in this particular case we have a product which has never been tried before.

The key factor in the application of probability theory to managerial decision is the common link of money. Even investments which are physically quite disparate have this common thread and we can, therefore, make a valid use of probability providing that we can view our decision as investments *of* money rather than *in* particular products or facilities. Naturally, the nature of the problem will strongly influence the particular probabilities arrived at but the theoretical justification for using Dr Harebrain's probabilities at all is that this decision is only one of many in the life of the company, not only new investments like this but also the frequent decisions on many other matters with uncertain outcomes.

The other justification is that the numbers should be in some sense 'right'. The only way in which we could be sure they were correct would be to launch many new products and, after the fact, see what proportion turned out to be low, medium, or high. Carrying out experiments like that just to test Dr Harebrain's probabilities would take a long time and could prove a very expensive undertaking. It would, however, be very useful to keep records of what the probabilities were expected to be and how the event turned out. If this was done as a matter of course, with due allowance for the changing business environment, it would provide a very valuable source of information for assessing future probabilities—rather on the lines of the car data.

In practice we have to assess these probabilities before the event and this may prove to be a very valuable exercise. There are many ways of assessing probabilities, e.g., by market research, opinion polling, test marketing, engineering studies, pilot-plant trials, laboratory experiments, analysing available data from economic statistics, analysing one's own past records, and so on. One of the most widely used methods is to write down a set of numbers and declare one's confidence in them. This seems very unscientific, but it then enables everyone else to attack them. They can then be invited to substitute their own assessment of the odds which can itself be debated. At the end of this process one has a set of probabilities which reflect the collective assessment of the decision-making group. Data from other sources such as opinion polls can be incorporated (using methods to be examined in a later chapter).

Arriving at probabilities by committee seems very strange but it is precisely what happens informally in any case. This time it is open, clear, and unambiguous.

Having discussed some of the justifications for, and implications of, using probability theory, we will illustrate in the rest of the book how it can be used. We shall, however, interject comments on repeatability and justification from time to time to remind the reader of the importance of these problems.

2.10 Conclusion

This chapter has necessarily been a brief summary of some of the fundamentals of probability theory. The main interest of the book lies in later chapters so the reader should concentrate on mastering the terminology rather than the formulae and be prepared to refer back to the appropriate section as the need arises. The reader who seeks a deeper understanding of probability may refer to *Probability and Statistics for Business Decision* by Robert Schlaifer or to my *Mathematics for Business Decisions*.

Problems

1. Events A, B, C, and D are collectively exhaustive and mutually exclusive. The probability distribution is

$$P(A) = 0.2, \quad P(A) = 0.1, \quad P(C) = 0.4$$

What is $P(D)$? Find $P(A \cup C)$, $P(A \cup B)$, $P(A \cup C \cup D)$. What are the probabilities of the compound events $(A \cup D)$, $(B \cup D)$, $(B \cup C \cup A)$?

2. In problem 1 what is the conditional probability that Event A occurred given that (A or C) was known to have happened but one did not know which? What is $P(B|(B \cup A \cup D))$?

3. In problem 1 suppose that the probabilities refer to the four possible outcomes of a test on a piece of material (e.g., that hardness falls in one of four ranges). If we test two successive pieces the event $(A \cap B)$ could denote that the first piece was in range A *and* the second was in range B.
  Find $P(A \cap B)$, $P(A \cap C \cap D)$, $P(A \cap A)$, $P(A \cap A \cap B)$, $P(A \cap B \cap C \cap D)$.

4. (a) Two events X and Y depend on each other in the sense that if X happens there is a 30% chance that Y will happen later on. If the probability of X is 60% what is the probability of both X and Y being observed?
  (b) After some time has passed it is observed that both X and Y happen about 25% of the time. Y is observed to follow X on about 30% of the occurrences of X. What can you infer about the probability of X?
  (c) You are now told that $P(X \cap Y)$ has risen to 0.40 while $P(Y|X)$ is still 0.30. What has happened?

5. Suppose that A, B, and C are events which are not mutually exclusive or collectively exhaustive and that $P(A) = 0.4$, $P(B) = 0.3$, $P(C) = 0.2$. What are $P(A \cup B)$, $P(B \cup C)$ and $P(A \cup B \cup C)$?

6. Try to draw up a list of situations from your own firm where the assumption of repeatability would be tenable and untenable. What would you do in the situations where there is no clear indication of whether the assumption can or cannot be made but you must still make a decision in the face of uncertainty.

3

Bayes' strategies

3.1 Introduction

In Chapter 1 we said that we needed to develop means by which best, or optimal strategies or actions could be selected taking into account our expectations about the various possible outcomes. The optimal strategy, incorporating probabilities, is called the **Bayes strategy**. The name is that of Thomas Bayes, one of the founders of the mathematical theory of gambling who, as Professor Moore has observed, had the rather unlikely occupation of Anglican Clergyman. For our purposes, the phrase 'Bayes' strategy' is merely a matter of using the accepted terminology.

3.2 Expected pay off

Suppose there is some action A which will be followed by one of two outcomes, I or II. Let the pay off from the first outcome be denoted by V_1 and from the second by V_2 (we use V for value rather than P for pay off because P is a recognized symbol for probability. This arrangement was made by mathematicians who are thought to be uninterested in money).

Further, let $P(\text{I})$ and $P(\text{II})$ be the respective probabilities of outcomes I and II. Then we define the expected pay off or expected value of action A to be

$$EV(A) = P(\text{I}) \times V_1 + P(\text{II}) \times V_2$$

In figures, if outcome I has a pay off of 100 and a probability of 60% or 0·60 and II has a pay off of 10 and a probability of 0·40 the expected value of A will be

$$0{\cdot}60 \times 100 + 0{\cdot}40 \times 10 = 64$$

or

$$EV(A) = 64$$

The symbols on the left-hand side of the equals sign are read 'expected value of A'.

This does not mean that if we choose A we shall receive 64 because obviously we shall receive 100 *or* we shall receive 10 and receiving 64 is impossible. What it does mean is that in a reasonably long series of actions if we consistently did A we should receive an *average* of 64 per action.

Now in most cases of managerial interest the decision problem in which the action A appears simply is not a member of a long identical series but, if we want to make use of the theory of probability, we have to be prepared to proceed as though it were. At the very least we have to be willing to treat this decision problem as one of a series which, although not identical in physical terms of factories, products, machines, etc., is almost identical with others to make it possible for us to rely on the notion of repeatability which was used in Chapter 2. If we are unwilling to do this or if it is unreasonable to do so then we shall be relying on a theory which is invalid and this may lead us to serious error. The whole problem is eased by the common factor of cash which we use to evaluate decision problems.

We shall return to this issue in Chapter 9 after we have explained some of the ramifications and more sophisticated aspects of decision theory. By that time the reader will have more of an idea of what use decision theory can be to him and will be better placed to judge whether the price he is forced to pay by the assumptions he has to make is worth the benefit he is likely to get. The choice of whether or not to use a particular theory in real-world problems is as much a decision problem as any other.

After that digression we point out that the formula used to define expected value applies equally regardless of how many outcomes there are and whether their pay offs are positive or negative. The only proviso is that they must be collectively exhaustive and mutually exclusive, that their probabilities must add to 1·0 (which is the same thing), and that none of the probabilities may be negative. In theory, probabilities can never be negative, but occasionally arithmetical error brings in one that is.

To illustrate the ideas of expected value suppose that action A has outcomes I to IV with pay offs and probabilities of:

Outcome	Pay off	Probability	
I	100	0·10	
II	− 60	0·40	
III	90	0·30	
IV	0	0·20	
		1·00	Check

The expected value of A will be

$$\text{EV(A)} = 0·10 \times 100 + 0·40 \times (-60) + 0·30 \times 90 + 0·20 \times 0$$
$$= 10 - 24 + 27 + 0$$
$$= 13$$

Care is needed with signs, and negative pay offs and their signs are best put in brackets to identify them. The rules are:

1 Check that the probabilities add to 1·00.

2 Multiply each pay off by its probability.

3 Add these products, taking account of the sign.

The idea of expected value can be applied equally well to the calculation of expected opportunity loss.

We can now calculate Bayes' strategies for a few problems, which we have already solved in Chapter 1.

The Hopeless Transport Company

In the Hopeless Transport Company's first problem they assign probabilities to the low and high maintenance needs as:

		Low	High
Vehicle	A	0·90	0·10
	B	0·60	0·40

The probabilities are different for actions A and B but both give a total of 1·00 when low and high are added. Adding down the columns is meaningless. The pay off table was:

		Outcome	
		High	Low
Action	A	10	15
	B	8	20

so the two expected values are

$$EV(A) = 10 \times 0·10 + 15 \times 0·90$$
$$= 14·5$$
$$EV(B) = 8 \times 0·40 + 20 \times 0·60$$
$$= 15·2$$

The expected value of B is larger than that of A, so the Bayes strategy would be to buy B. This is not the same as the maximin pay off strategy because we have allowed for the probability of the higher pay off from choice B and outcome II.

Mass Marketing Ltd—expected value

In this case, we shall assume that the outcome is independent of the action chosen. For example, the three outcomes might be the development of three different levels of population which would be independent of which product was being marketed (except, perhaps for a particular type of product).

The outcomes are estimated by Mass Marketing Ltd to have probabilities of 0·20, 0·40, and 0·40 so we can incorporate these values into the pay off table.

		Outcome			EV of action
		I	II	III	
Probability		0·20	0·40	0·40	
	A	20	40	30	32
Action	B	80	70	− 10	40
	C	90	10	− 20	14
	D	10	100	40	58

The reader should verify this result.

The highest EV is for Action D and that is the optimal act or Bayes' strategy. Using maximin it was action A.

Mass Marketing—opportunity losses

We use the same probabilities and the opportunity loss table and calculate expected opportunity losses (EOL). The Bayes strategy is the one with the **minimum EOL**

The table now is:

		Outcome			EOL
		I	II	III	
Probability		0·20	0·40	0·40	
	A	70	60	10	42
Action	B	10	30	50	34
	C	0	90	60	60
	D	80	0	0	16

The minimum EOL is now for action D and that is the Bayes strategy for this criterion.

We now have a slightly confusing situation as four criteria have given three different answers.

Criterion	Indicated action	
Maximin pay off	A	
Minimax opportunity loss	B	
Maximum EV	D	Bayes' strategy
Minimum EOL	D	Bayes' strategy

The last two answers are Bayes' strategies because they incorporate probabilities while the first two are not.

We evinced no surprise when the first two criteria gave different answers in Chapter 1, though they gave the same answer in the Hopeless Transport Company's second problem. However, the last two criteria now lead to the same conclusion. Is this coincidence or is there some more fundamental reason?

It is a very important result that it can be proved mathematically that Bayes' strategies are always the same for maximum expected value and minimum expected opportunity loss. This only applies to Bayes' strategies where the probabilities feature in the calculation. In practice, it means that we can use pay off or opportunity loss interchangeably provided that we also include the probabilities in whichever calculation we elect to do. Since the entries in the COL table are always zero or positive it generally makes life simpler to use that because there is less chance of confusing signs. We have to remember that there may be nothing but losses involved in the recommended action so that we need to be sure that the problem has been defined properly.

A simple version of the mathematical proof is given in Appendix A for the benefit of those readers who like such things. It is not necessary to understand the proof in order to follow the rest of the book.

The Hopeless Transport Company and dummy acts
We can now show how the inclusion of dummy actions into a pay off table leads to the correct result when probabilities are included. By 'correct' we mean a result which accords with common sense though that is not always the best guide. If it were, there would be no need for decision theory.

In Section 1.7 we have a pay off table for three outcomes and four actions including a dummy. Suppose the probabilities for the three outcomes have been stipulated by management to be 0·50, 0·25, and 0·25 respectively so we can now calculate expected values as follows:

		Outcome			EV
		I	II	III	
		0·50	0·25	0·25	
Probability					
	A	− 80	− 40	− 5	− 51·25
Action	B	− 30	− 20	− 15	− 23·75
	C	− 90	− 10	− 10	− 50
	D	0	0	0	0

Action D has the highest EV and is therefore the Bayes strategy. The reader should now work the problem for himself using COL and confirm that the EOL's are 51·25, 23·75, 50, and 0 so that D is still the Bayes strategy.

Problems

1. There are four outcomes with the following pay offs and probabilities.

Outcome	Pay off	Probability
I	25	0·40
II	− 40	0·20
III	16	0·20
IV	− 8	0·20

What is the expected value?

2. There is a strong degree of agreement in the company that the first two probabilities in Problem 1 are correct but there is bitter disagreement about the last two. You resolve to calculate the probability which outcome III should have in order to make the expected value of the project just positive.

3. What are the implications of the last problem?

4. What are the expected value and expected opportunity loss for the pay off table?

		Outcome			
		I	II	III	IV
Probability		0·40	0·20	0·30	0·10
	A	60	80	150	110
Action	B	70	95	165	120
	C	90	80	190	70

5. Carry out a sensitivity analysis on the last problem.

6. In problem 1 of Chapter 1 the company has assessed probabilities of 0·4, 0·2, and 0·4 for outcomes I, II, and III respectively. Find the maximum EV (and thus the minimum EOL) strategy.

7. In problem 6 what happens to the solution if the probabilities are changed to 0·5, 0·4, and 0·1 for outcomes I, II, and III respectively?

4

Decision trees

4.1 Sequential problems

Many managerial problems have a rather long-drawn-out structure in that they consist of a whole sequence of actions and outcomes. For example, in a new product development programme, the first action is often test-marketing and the action choice might be between intensive and gradual testing. Having taken this decision there is an outcome—perhaps the product reception is favourable, fair, or poor. Given one of these outcomes—fair, say—one then has to decide between redesigning the product, an advertising campaign, or withdrawing altogether. Given that decision, there will be an outcome which leads to another decision, and so on.

There are two important features to this kind of decision problem—time and uncertainty. In the real world each of these actions and outcomes takes some time to initiate or unfold. In total, the elapsed time may be very large. The effects of time on financial values can be incorporated very well by discounting, but the probabilities in the problem may also be influenced by the passage of time and the emergence of more information. In Chapter 6 we shall investigate Bayes' theorem which allows us to modify probabilities in the light of further information.

The other factor is that uncertainty is made more severe by being compounded into a chain of events. It is hard enough to make an assessment of probabilities in the case of a single action with several outcomes but it is much more difficult to make a set of mutually consistent probability assessments for a whole chain of outcomes. However, we defer detailed consideration of this problem to the last chapter. For the moment, we merely observe that, despite the difficulties involved, the manager has to solve these problems *in any case*. Regardless of whether or not he writes anything down, uses formulae, or has ever heard of Bayes' strategies, he is balancing uncertainty in some way. The contention of modern decision theory is that it is better to have some formal procedure for dealing with uncertainty because that at least makes managerial judgement explicit and open to discussion by those involved.

Having said that complex decision problems have a sequential structure it seems fairly obvious to represent them by diagrams which show the branching ramifications of the decision and outcomes involved. These diagrams are called **decision trees** and we now consider ways in which they can be constructed and conclusions drawn from them.

4.2 Mass Marketing Ltd

Mass Marketing Ltd has a new wonder product of which they expect great things. At the moment they have two courses of action open to them. To test market it or abandon it. If they test it, it will cost £100 000 and the response could be positive or negative with probabilities of 0·60 and 0·40. If it is positive they could either abandon the product or market it full scale. If they market full scale the result might be low, medium, or high demand, and the respective net pay offs would be − 200, 200, or 1000 in units of £1000 (i.e., the result could range from a net loss of £200 000 to a gain of £1 000 000). These outcomes have probabilities of 0·20, 0·50, and 0·30 respectively.

If the result of the test marketing is negative they have decided to abandon the product. If, at any point, they abandon it there is a net gain of £50 000 from the sale of scrap. All the financial values have been discounted to the present.

This description is already quite long and it will be easily appreciated that the problem has been drastically simplified. Despite this it is by no means easy to see from the description what Mass Marketing Ltd should do.

Figure 4.1 is the tree diagram for the problem and the reader should study the diagram in the light of the ensuing explanation of its notation.

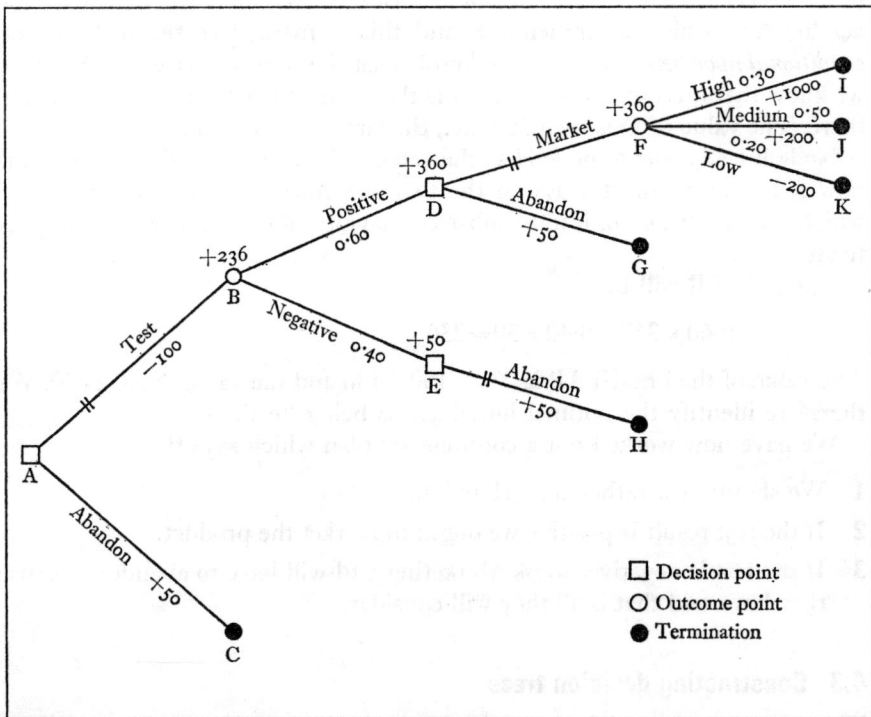

Fig. 4.1 Decision tree for Mass Marketing Ltd

The squares on the diagram are points at which decisions have to be made, the circles are points at which one of a number of outcomes may occur, and

CDA

the dots are the end of chains of events. These points are collectively called **nodes**.

The 'branches' between the nodes are either decisions or outcomes and each is labelled with an identification, a probability, or a value where appropriate. For convenience of explanation each node is labelled. The numbers written above the nodes are expected values and the lines drawn across some of the branches (—┤├—), show optimal paths. These are located in the following way.

We start at the right-hand edge of the diagram and trace each branch back to its source. We may use any criterion but in this example we use maximum expected values. Thus, nodes I, J, and K are reached from node F as a result of a probabilistic outcome in the sense that, having reached node F, there is no means of knowing where we will end up except that it will be one of I, J, or K. The EV for node F is therefore calculated in exactly the usual way as

$$0\cdot30 \times 1000 + 0\cdot50 \times 200 + 0\cdot20 \times (-200) = +360$$

and this value is written above node F.

Nodes G and F are reached from D, and at D we can choose which node to move to and D is a decision point. If we choose to move to G there will be a certain payment of £50 000 (or +50) and if we choose to move to F there will be an expected value of 360. As our criterion is maximum EV we choose the act 'market' which is branch DF and this is marked as the optimal act, *conditional upon being at* D. As we know what the optimal act would be at D, we know that the value of being at D is the value of what we can get by being there. The value of D is then 360, i.e., the larger of 360 and 50.

Node E leads only to node H so the value of E is 50. The value of node B is now found by taking the EV of the two outcomes 'positive' and 'negative' which, as we have seen, lead to sub-trees having values of 360 and 50 respectively.

The EV of B will be

$$0\cdot60 \times 360 + 0\cdot40 \times 50 = 236$$

The value of the branch AB is $236 - 100 = 136$ and the value of AC is 50. We therefore identify the optimal initial act as being 'test'.

We have now worked out a contingency plan which says that:

1 We should test rather than abandon.

2 If the test result is positive we ought to market the product.

3 If the test is negative, Mass Marketing Ltd will have to abandon because they have said that is all they will consider.

4.3 Constructing decision trees

There are no universal formulae for constructing decision trees because each one is tailored to an individual problem and its branches are as long and complex or short and simple as needed (the reader will already have noticed that the branches may be of different lengths if need be). We can, however, offer a few rules of thumb.

1 Use a fairly large piece of paper as the tree will almost certainly wander off a small one.

2 Divide it up from left to right into a series of vertical strips for actions and outcomes. Make the strips a couple of inches wide and allow for more than you think you will need. It is often useful to label these strips 'action', 'outcome', 'action', 'outcome', and so on, across the bottom of the sheet.

3 Start at the left-hand edge with a decision box, recalling that there are nearly always at least two possible decisions—'do something' and 'do nothing', e.g., 'test' and 'abandon' in the Mass Marketing Ltd case.

4 Try to follow each branch in turn across the page, writing down only the labels of actions and outcomes for a start. This process will, in itself, often stimulate new ideas for actions, a phenomenon which is at least half and probably much more of the value of the decision-tree technique.

5 When the tree is complete try to get someone to check it for omissions.

6 Now write down the probabilities. In a real-world situation this is a very salutary experience and you may find that you really have no idea of what the likelihoods of the various outcomes are. This is again a very useful practical feature of the tree because it may save you from blundering ahead with an action. There is a very real temptation to say 'the tree technique is useless because we don't know what the probabilities are'. This is putting the cart before the horse with a vengeance. Decision trees and the other techniques of decision theory are not intended to be number-crunching masters which have to be obeyed and fed with raw material. If the probabilities cannot be assigned to some particular set of outcomes then this means that you are in a situation where you are about to launch into the future with *no* idea of what is likely to happen. This is bad managerial practice not impractical managerial theory.

7 Working from right to left calculate the EVs and determine the optimal acts at each decision stage. Remember to verify that the probabilities on the branches from each outcome node do add up to 1.00.

8 Ensure that the whole thing makes some kind of sense, with due caution about relying too heavily on intuition in these very complex cases.

9 Even if the recommended strategies do make sense in the real world, but especially if they do not, recheck the probabilities. If in doubt, recalculate the tree with different probabilities and see how and where the optimal acts change. If you have to change the probabilities by fairly large amounts before the optimal path becomes different then you have a fairly robust tree and the problem is fairly clearcut. In many cases, however, there will be a point in the tree where quite small alterations in the probabilities will make fairly large changes in the optimal path, even reaching right back to the starting point because of the changed expected values. If this happens it focuses attention on the critical area and usually indicates the need for more study by, for example, market research methods.

10 Finally, don't get too involved with the tree technique itself. It depends on probabilities and these are nearly always a matter of someone's opinion about what is likely to happen in the future. This does not invalidate the method because managerial decisions generally depend on someone's opinion (usually referred to as his 'considered judgement'). The great value of decision trees is that they bring these opinions into the open where they can be scrutinized for what they are as long as you are not too busy drawing squares and circles.

This section probably makes decision trees seem an incredible amount of work. They are not but, like everything else, the first few take much longer than the later ones. With a little practice a tree can be written down directly from knowledge of the problem and can be amended as the sequence of events unfolds.

At this point the reader should turn back to the beginning of Section 4.2 and, without looking at Fig. 4.1, try to draw Mass Marketing Ltd's Decision Tree from the problem description.

4.4 Another example—the Heath Robinson Engineering Company

We shall now test the methods we have developed in this chapter by describing and solving a more complicated problem. Before looking at the solution, the reader may wish to try to solve the problem himself to try out his skill.

The Heath Robinson Engineering Company has a long and successful record of building a variety of heavy-duty materials-handling equipment. Their new Managing Director has been extensively trained in decision theory and other modern management methods and is leading the company into new fields of endeavour. One possibility open to them is to develop and market ground-handling equipment for a new supersonic helicopter which is being built by an international consortium. Many airlines have already agreed to buy the helicopter and there will be a heavy demand for ground-handling equipment of which the Heath Robinson Engineering Company could expect to gain a share, providing their design is successful. The main uncertainty is when the helicopter will be in service. The most informed estimates are divided between 1 year, 5 years, and 10 years hence, the various proportions being 10%, 60%, and 30% (i.e., 10% of commentators say 1 year, etc.). By dint of a little work with DCF tables, the Heath Robinson Engineering Company have worked out that the present value of their receipts from these outcomes would be (in monetary units):

Market develops in	Present value of receipts (m.u.)
1 year	200
5 years	125
10 years	80

The design and development costs are estimated to be 50 m.u. At the moment, the chances of success are not too good as the Heath Robinson Engineering Company are new in this field and would have to use existing motor and hydraulic equipment. They feel that the chance of building a successful machine if they start now will be only about 60%.

There are, however, a number of alternatives. They could abandon the whole idea now or they could wait a year and see what has happened to the helicopter. If it is in service by then, they could develop their machine at a cost of 45 m.u. (present value) but they would miss out on much of the market by being late and the present value of their receipts would be reduced to 120 m.u. (Receipts are income less direct expenditure excluding development costs.) Waiting a year would improve their chances of developing a successful machine to 70% because more would be known about the helicopter, and the task the ground-handling equipment had to do.

If the helicopter had not reached service at the end of 1 year, the Heath Robinson Engineering Company could either abandon the project or wait for another 3 years. At the end of the 3 years, improved motors and hydraulics together with the data which could be obtained by a prolonged study of aircraft handling problems would practically guarantee a successful design, say a 90% chance of success. However, after the three more years the chance of the high gain from the helicopter coming into use 1 year from now would have passed and the helicopter could only come into service at either the 5-year or 10-year points from now.

After the 3-year additional wait, the Heath Robinson Engineering Company would still have the option of abandoning the whole project. Against this, the effect of waiting a total of 4 years before starting on development reduces the present value of the development costs to 35 m.u. The collection of the additional design information and licensing on the improved motors and hydraulics would cost 10 m.u.

Despite the simplifications which have been made, this is a very complicated problem and it is by no means evident from the problem description just what actions the Heath Robinson Engineering Company should take.

The reader is invited to try to solve the problem. A full solution is given in Appendix B. There are a couple of points which are worth noting before attempting the solution.

Although the normal sequence of branches in a decision tree is 'action—response—action—response' etc., it is perfectly legitimate to have successive response branches. In this tree, it is necessary to have them. The other point is that the probabilities on the response branches from a particular node have to add to 1·00. For instance, when the chance of the helicopter coming into service in 1 year has passed there are only two remaining possibilities, – 5 years and 10 years. The original probabilities for these two outcomes have to be scaled up to make them add to 1·00.

As this example is really a problem there are no formal problems in this chapter. The real practice comes from recognizing decision-tree problems in real life. Once the problem has been recognized the arithmetic is easy.

5

Utility

5.1 The limitations of expected value

Throughout the book so far we have relied heavily on the concept of expected value or, in full, expected monetary value (EMV), in order to allow us to combine probabilities and money in the analysis of decisions. It must be said, however, that there are situations in which EMV has grave weaknesses, so grave in fact that we are obliged to develop a new idea to overcome them. This idea is that of **utility** and it is explored in this chapter but first we need to analyse the weaknesses of EMV.

Suppose that a decision-maker (DM) is invited to invest in a project which, if successful, offers a net benefit of £100 000 but which if it fails will lead to a net loss of £200 000. The probability of success is estimated to be 0·80 so the EMV of the project is

$$0 \cdot 80 \times 100\,000 + 0 \cdot 20 \times (-200\,000) = £40\,000$$

The EMV is positive so the project is better than doing nothing and if that is the only alternative then EMV indicates that the DM should accept the proposal and undertake the project. This is simply another example of the standard method we have used so far in the book.

Now, suppose that the DM controls a relatively small business to which a loss of £200 000 would mean a complete, utter, and irretrievable catastrophe but which is not in such a desperate situation that it would fail if no action was taken. Thus, the DM is not completely desperate for the £100 000 but he simply could not contemplate the loss of £200 000. The measure of EMV indicates that he ought to go ahead but the circumstances are such that this is obviously the wrong indication.

Suppose now that the same DM in the same corporate circumstances was offered a project with the same odds of success but with pay offs and losses only one-tenth of the previous project. The EMV is

$$0 \cdot 80 \times 10\,000 + 0 \cdot 20 \times (-20\,000) = £4000$$

If the financial situation is such that a loss of £20 000 would be no more than an irritation then the EMV measure of the project indicates that it should be undertaken and this will be correct.

We now have a company for which EMV sometimes gives the right answer and sometimes does not. How do we resolve this paradox?

The key lies in the magnitude of the losses which might be incurred. For this company, a loss of £200 000 leads to total failure and this is somehow more than ten times as bad as a loss of £20 000. There is a biological parallel to this. If a person's body temperature rises by 2°F this indicates a slight fever but if it rises by 20°F the person will die. The second temperature rise is ten times as large as the first but the consequences are more than ten times as serious. Even ten successive slight fevers, each followed by a return to normality, will not be the same as one death just as ten losses of £20 000, providing there is time to recoup them, will not be as bad as one loss of £200 000 because such a loss would lead to bankruptcy and there could be no chance of recovering from that.

Clearly, we could avoid the whole situation by returning to the measurement of minimax loss which we used in Chapter 1 but as we pointed out, that criterion took no account of probability so we should be no better off. The ideal thing to do is not to abandon EMV but to adapt it so that it will always work and we do this by bringing in the concept of utility.

5.2 Monetary units and conversion charts

The principles underlying utility are really rather simple. Recall, that in earlier parts of the book we have worked not with £ but with arbitrary 'monetary units'—m.u. for short. This is really a matter of laziness. Suppose we had a problem in which the various sums of money were £100 000, £200 000, and − £400 000 then it saves a lot of work to choose a monetary unit of £100 000 and call the various amounts 1 m.u., 2 m.u., and − 4 m.u. With this conversion ratio, £175 000 would be 1·75 m.u., and so on. We can choose the conversion factor to suit the problem and the only proviso is that we have to state clearly what the conversion factor is in order to avoid ambiguity.

The conversion factor in no way alters the scale of the problem. Thus, with a scale of £20 000 = 1 m.u., − £20 000 would be − 1 m.u. and − £200 000 would be − 10 m.u., and the ratio of the two amounts remains at 10 to 1 regardless of whether they are measured in £ or m.u.

It might be convenient to draw up a chart or graph enabling amounts to be converted from £ to m.u., or back again, for any particular problem. For instance, we might have to deal with problems in which the amounts of money were nearly always between + £200 000 and − £100 000. Taking a conversion scale of £10 000 = 1 m.u. the amounts would be between 20 m.u. and − 10 m.u. These limits are plotted on a chart such as Fig. 5.1 (the points A and B) and a straight line is drawn to connect them. The result is, in effect, a pictorial conversion table from £ to m.u. and back again. The horizontal and vertical lines show how £55 000 is read off as 5·5 m.u. and − 6·2 m.u. is found to be − £62 000. These conversions could of course, be easily found by calculation and the chart is really an explanatory device. Obviously, these charts can be drawn for any range of £ and for any desired conversion factor.

A chart of this shape is called **'linear'** because the conversion line drawn on it is straight.

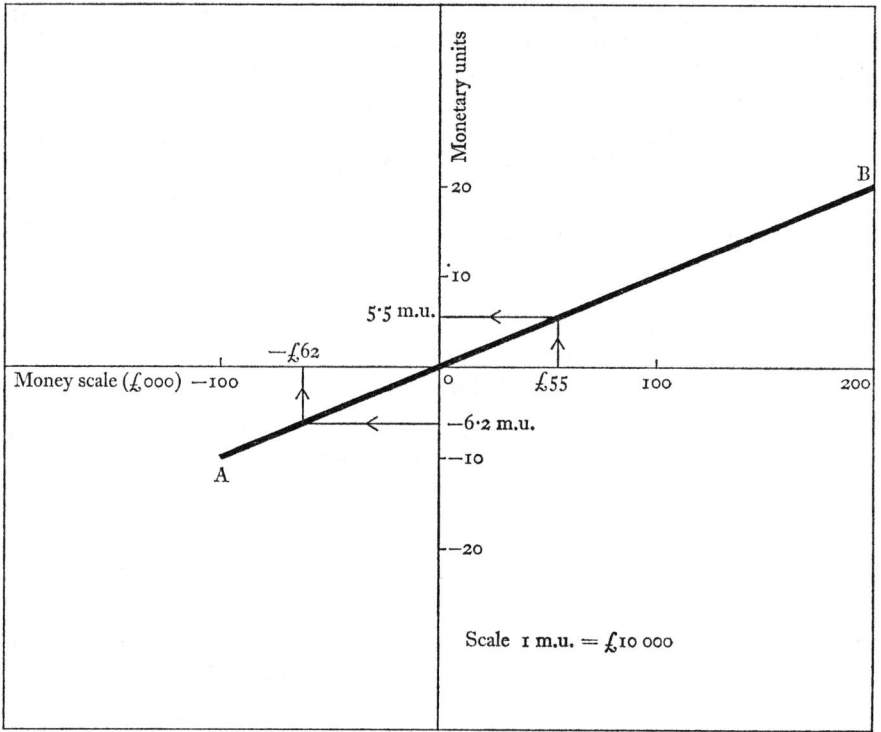

Fig. 5.1 Conversion chart: £ to monetary units

5.3 The idea of utility

We have said earlier that the DM, whose problem we analysed, wanted to be able to take account of the fact that a loss of £200 000 was more than ten times as bad as a loss of £20 000. Now, in principle, we could add to the loss of £200 000 all the lost profits due to going out of business and thus arrive at the true loss. This would make the total much larger than £200 000 and, therefore, much more than ten times as much as £20 000. The trouble is that it is impossible to estimate what these costs are, let alone to allow for the intangibles such as shame and loss of employment for the DM. However, the linear graph of Fig. 5.1 offers an insight into how we might allow for the more serious effect of larger losses without trying to estimate all the costs involved in bankruptcy or in trying to recover from very severe, but not quite fatal losses.

If we allow the line OA in Fig. 5.1 to depart from its original straight path and bend downwards ever more steeply as the losses get larger we could reach the point where, instead of − £100 000 being − 10 m.u. we could make it, say − 20 m.u. Suppose, we do not start bending the line until we have passed − £20 000 which we suppose to be the limit beyond which losses become very serious for the health of this particular business and therefore more than simply losses of money. We should reach the situation where − £10 000 is equated with − 1 unit and − £100 000 is regarded as − 20 units. The ratio of 10 to 1 when they are measured in £ has become 20 to 1 when they are measured in units. Perhaps $-£200000$ would become -100 units while $-£20000$ stayed at -2 units. This converts a 10 to 1 ratio in £ to 50 to 1 in units and this implies the DM's assessment of the consequences of going out of business. This is the essence of the idea of utility.

It would be as well not to make the curve bend down too steeply or to start the bending too quickly because this could lead us into the situation where we attached such enormously large importance to the possibility of loss that we never took any risks and therefore never made any gains. In this case, the business would fail in any case and we should have brought about the very situation we had sought so hard to avoid.

Perhaps the end result, for the loss-making side of the conversion chart, would be like Fig. 5.2. This new chart is said to be **nonlinear** because it is no

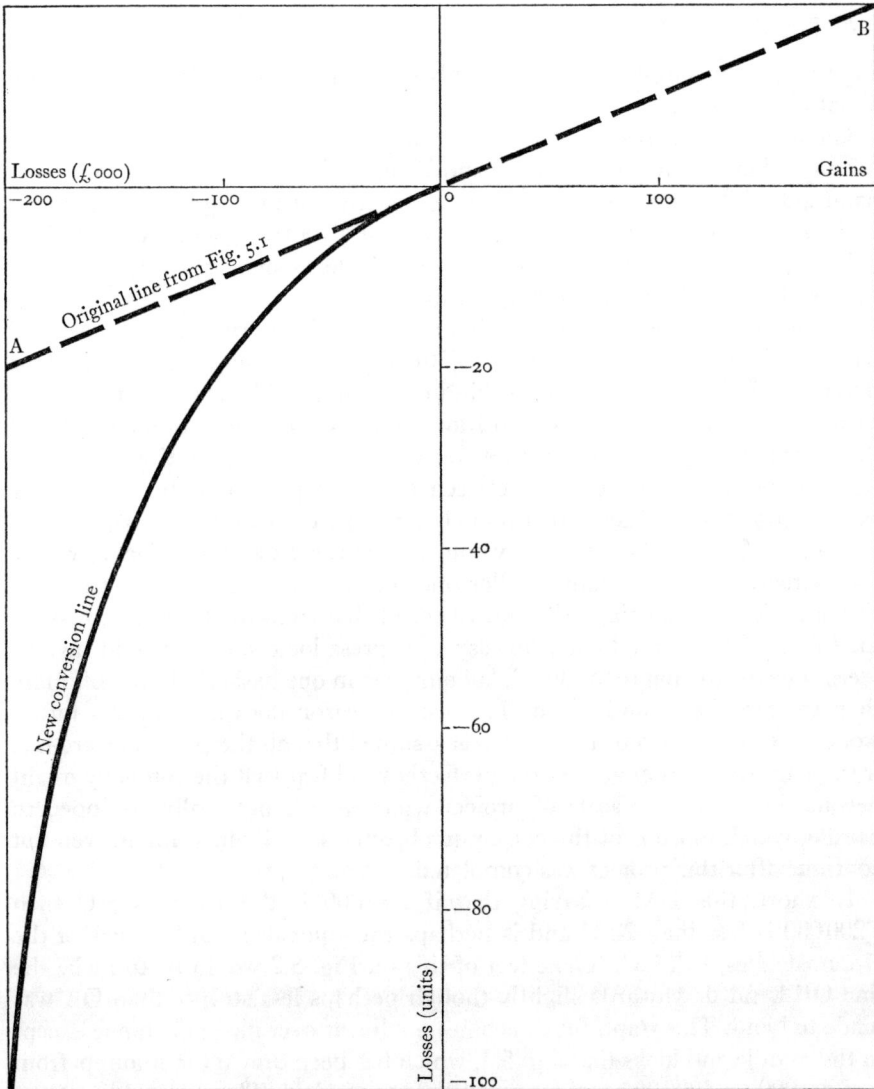

Fig. 5.2 Conversion chart modified for losses

longer a straight line. For this reason we can no longer quote a single conversion factor from £ to units because the rate of exchange varies from place to place on the chart.

The reader may have noticed that we have stopped referring to monetary units or m.u. and are now mentioning simply 'units'. This is because the new units are no longer of money only, they are 'money and other consequences'. In fact they are units of what is called utility because 'money and other consequences' is the same idea as 'money and the things we could utilize it for'. The new units are called **utils** by some writers but we shall merely refer to them as units and denote them by U to indicate that they are of utility.

5.4 Positive utility

Figure 5.2 is incomplete because it only covers the losses side of the picture. What about gains?

Gains can be expressed in U by sticking to the original conversion factor (or any other which is convenient) and keeping the graph linear on the right-hand side. This implies that we would regard a gain of £100 000 as being 10 U and a gain of £10 000 as being 1 U and £100 000 would be treated, in either £ or U, as being ten times as desirable as one of £10 000. Is this necessarily a valid way of looking at things?

Consider a business which usually involves itself in projects with potential pay offs of between + £50 000 and − £50 000 (a loss is a negative pay off). This business will be geared up to this kind of amount by the size and type of its managerial structure, the composition of its work force, purchasing and design staffs and, in short, its whole outlook and way of operating. Now, the business is offered the choice between one long project with a practically assured pay off of + £200 000 or four shorter ones each with a virtually certain pay off of £50 000. Many DMs would regard the £200 000 project as rather less attractive than the four smaller ones even though the pay off from the single project is financially the equivalent of that from the four. The reasons for this preference might not be easy to express logically but would involve ideas such as 'too big to swallow', 'all our eggs in one basket', 'biting off more than we can chew', and so on. The second reason does not imply a rather woolly idea of risk even though it was assumed that all the projects were risk free, or nearly so. It expresses the perfectly valid fear that the company might become involved in a scale of project which it was not really equipped to handle, which did not fit the corporate objectives, and which might well not continue after this project was completed.

In short, this DM is saying that if £50 000 is the same as 5 U then £200 000 is less than 20 U and is perhaps the equivalent, in his view of the circumstances, to 15 U. The effect of this on Fig. 5.2 would be to make the line OB bend downwards slightly though perhaps less steeply than OA was made to bend. The graph thus becomes nonlinear over its whole range except in the middle and looks like Fig. 5.3, which has been drawn for amounts from − £200 000 to £200 000 and from − 100 U to + 15 U. The original line from Fig. 5.1 is shown in Fig. 5.3 for purposes of comparison.

5.5 Shapes of utility curve

The utility curve does not have to be linear in its middle range and it can, in fact, be absolutely any shape which reflects the views of the DM. In fact, a utility curve could be perfectly linear just as Fig. 5.1 was. If it is, it implies that the DM feels that the sizes of the gain are neither so large as to be indigestible nor so negative as to be disastrous and he is quite content to take gains and losses as they turn out. In a sense, he is prepared to accept the odds as gamblers do in making small bets at a race meeting and a linear utility graph is often labelled 'playing the odds' but we shall call it **'risk-neutral'**.

A more usual shape for the curve is the one in Fig. 5.3. This, as we have

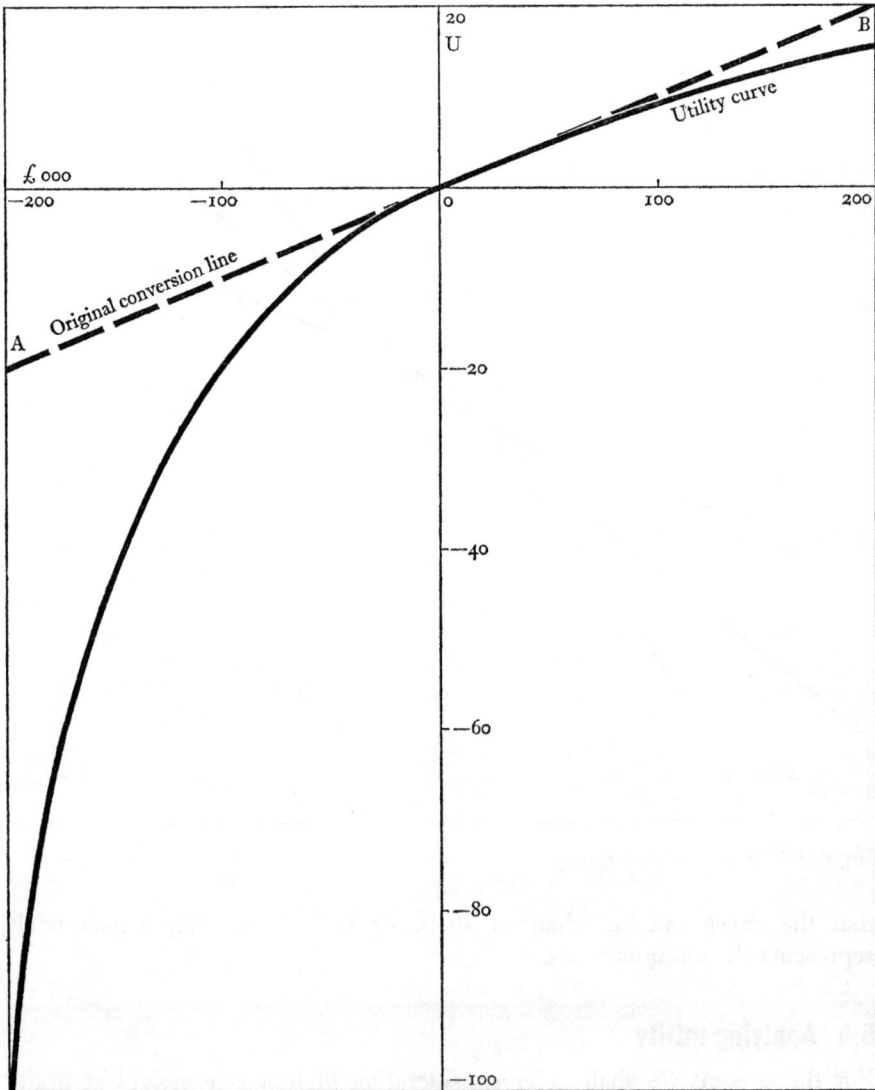

Fig. 5.3 Completed utility chart

argued, is that of a DM who avoids extremes and is called a **'risk-averse curve'**.

It would be possible to draw a curve which bent upwards rather than down. This corresponds to someone who prefers one large pay off to the financially equivalent number of small ones. The curve might belong to someone who was an addictive gambler or whose company was in such a plight that he was desperate for a large win. The curve is called **'risk-prone'** and would be unlikely in the modern corporation.

The three theoretical shapes are shown in Fig. 5.4 but it must be stressed

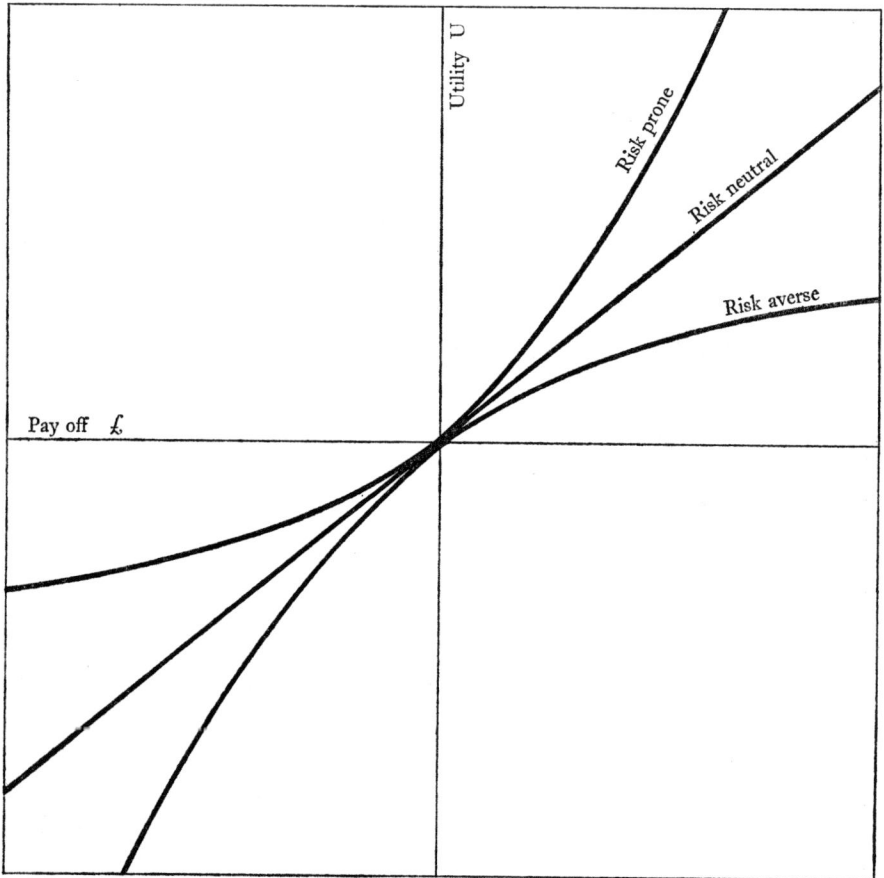

Fig. 5.4 The basic utility curves

that the curve can be whatever shape or mixture of shapes adequately represents the circumstances.

5.6 Applying utility

For the present we shall defer consideration of how one arrives at utility curves in practice and examine what is done with them when they have been obtained.

In Section 5.1 we considered a problem in which there were pay offs of £100 000 or − £200 000 with probabilities of 0·80 and 0·20 respectively. We calculated the expected monetary value as

$$\text{EMV} = 0·80 \times 100\,000 + 0·20 \times (-200\,000)$$
$$= £40\,000$$

Now, from Fig. 5.3 we can read off that

$$£100\,000 = 9 \text{ U} \quad \text{and} \quad -£200\,000 = -100 \text{ U}$$

Substituting these values into the equation for expected monetary value would give, by analogy, **expected utility** which would be

$$\text{E U} = 0·80 \times 9 + 0·20 \times (-100)$$
$$= -12·8 \text{ U}$$

Recall that the DM had the option of doing nothing, thus getting a pay off of £0 which clearly has a utility of zero, both logically and from Fig. 5.3. In the circumstances, and by applying the criterion of maximum expected utility in place of the standard one of maximum EMV, the DM would prefer to do nothing and would decline to participate in the project. This is what his fear of a loss of £200 000 indicated that he should do, therefore, the use of expected utility has led to the right decision.

Utility is, therefore, used in exactly the same way as money in the analysis, whether the method is maximin pay off, decision trees, or any other technique.

The decision-maker could, of course, adopt the rule of never getting involved in any project with possible serious consequences. If he does he will not be taking account of the likelihood of the favourable outcome and will be bound to forego some very tempting projects. In short, he will probably be taking a much too conservative and defensive view of life and his business will be unlikely to prosper greatly. Naturally, he will probably be right in avoiding projects where the unfavourable outcome would be literally ruinous but such projects do not arise all that frequently and a properly drawn utility curve will automatically keep them out by bringing in such large negative utilities that even a very small probability for the unfavourable outcome cannot make the expected utility go positive.

At this point the energetic reader may find it useful to invent a few different utility curves and then use them to rework some of the earlier problems in the book, perhaps doing the problem with a few different sets of probabilities for each utility curve. This will give a better understanding of the combined effects of utility and probability than any number of pages of description and analysis.

5.7 Drawing utility curves

Having discussed at some length what a utility curve is, and how it is used, it would be useful to consider how they are arrived at in practice.

There are at least two general methods of reaching a utility curve reflecting the decision-maker's preference. Both start at the same point and they then diverge considerably in technique, though the end result should be the same.

The first stage is to decide what person or group the curve is to represent and to decide on the size of the pay offs usually involved in their decision making. The scale of decision and the factors to be weighed vary from level to level in the company and probably across the lower levels as well. Each decision-making point in the company should in principle have its own utility curve though they might be portions from some overall corporate curve. Certainly the curve for The Board of I.C.I. should not be the same as that of The Works Manager of its smallest factory. The Board's curve might have to cover a range from $-£10\,000\,000$ to $+£100\,000\,000$ while The Works Manager's may go from $-£10\,000$ to $£100\,000$. The two curves would need different horizontal scales, the latter being more detailed than the former. The Board might need several curves for different sizes of decision.

Generally, for a given company the curves for the large decisions would tend to be risk-averse in shape while the small-decision curves would get closer to the risk-neutral position. It could in fact be argued, though the idea may seem a little revolutionary, that the directors of a company should largely confine their activities to drawing utility curves for themselves and their subordinate decision-makers and issuing revised curves when, in their judgement, changes in business conditions warrant it. Whether the idea that the boardroom need be equipped only with a pad of graph paper will catch on remains to be seen.

Having decided, then, on the horizontal scale for the graph one chooses a suitable value for the maximum point on the scale for U and at this point the methods for drawing the actual shape of the curve diverge. They can be called the statistician's and the pragmatist's methods.

The statistician's method starts from the fact that it is theoretically possible to express a point on a utility curve as a lottery. The DM is asked a series of questions such as 'there is a gamble (or project) which will have a pay off of $+£200\,000$ or $-£200\,000$. What probability of success would make you just indifferent about whether to undertake the project or not?' The DM replies, for example, that at an 87% chance of success he would be indifferent about the project.

If the value $15\,U$ has been chosen to represent $£200\,000$ we can now calculate what the DM's probability statement implies about his assessment of the utility of $-£200\,000$. We let X stand for the unknown utility of $-£200\,000$ and the DM's probability statement says the expected utility of the project is

$$0\cdot87 \times 15 + 0\cdot13 \times X$$

The 15 is the utility of $£200\,000$ which was chosen as a starting point for the utility scale and the $0\cdot87$ and $0\cdot13$ are the two probabilities—the first being given by the DM and the second calculated from it.

Now, this expected utility has to be zero because the DM said that when the probability was 87% he would be indifferent about whether he did the project or not. Therefore,

$$0\cdot87 \times 15 + 0\cdot13 \times X = 0$$

or

$$X = \frac{-0.87 \times 15}{0.13}$$

$$= -100 \quad \text{(very nearly)}$$

The whole point of this process is to draw a curve like that in Fig. 5.3 and we now have three points on it, namely,

$$£200\,000 = 15 \text{ U}$$
$$£0 = 0 \text{ U}$$
$$-£200\,000 = -100 \text{ U}$$

Three points are not sufficient to define the curve fully and the statistician's method requires the DM to answer more questions of the same type but with the values chosen to fill in the vacant points on the graph. When enough points (at the very least six or eight for Fig. 5.3) have been obtained, a smooth curve is fitted to them either free-hand or by some statistical procedure and that becomes the utility curve.

Where this procedure has been tried in practice and the results have been published the curve has not been the smooth shape of Fig. 5.3 but has tended to wander about. This is because it is practically impossible for the DM to give perfectly consistent answers all the time, especially when the questions are phrased rather hypothetically.

The approach used by the pragmatist is drastically simpler than this. He chooses a horizontal scale of money and a conversion factor which he thinks is suitable and then draws a simple conversion chart like Fig. 5.1. He then takes a coloured pencil and boldly draws a free-hand utility curve by looking at the linear conversion chart and making the curve as nonlinear as he thinks is proper.

This procedure has the merits of simplicity, decisiveness, and speed but is open to the objection that it is a little too glib.

The ideal procedure is of course a cross between the two and could be called the pragmatic statistician's approach. Take a few (four say) actual past projects which are reasonably typical of the type of business you do. Convert the financial data into present-day prices. Now, ask the question 'under today's business conditions what chance of success would these projects have to have before we would be just willing to embark on them?'. Doing a few calculations like those in the statistician's method will give several points on the curve, to be exact the number of projects considered plus the point £0 = 0 U and this will serve to give the general shape of the graph.

Now, take a couple of current projects and convert their financial values into U from the graph. You can now calculate the success probability at which the utility curve implies you should be indifferent about doing the project. This is called an **indifference probability** and this can be illustrated using Fig. 5.3 to represent the utility curve resulting from the analysis of the past projects.

Suppose one of the new projects has potential pay offs of +£200 000 and −£100 000. From Fig. 5.3 these are 15 U and −20 U respectively. Let the indifference probability of success be denoted by P, then at this probability the expected utility of the project is zero and we have

$$EU = 0 = P \times 15 + (100 - P) \times (-20)$$

i.e.,

$$15P - 20 \times 100 + 20P = 0$$
$$35P = 2000$$

$$P = \frac{2000}{35} = 57\%$$

If P was taken as a decimal the initial expression would be

$$EV = 0 = P \times 15 + (1 - P) \times (-20)$$

so

$$P = 0 \cdot 57$$

the same result.

The utility graph thus says that this project should be undertaken if the chance of success is more than 57% but not if it is less than 57%. If this is in agreement with our judgement then the utility curve is correct (though we shall check it for another new project just to be sure). If it is not, we adjust the curve until it does give satisfactory results.

This all seems rather elaborate and time consuming. Like anything else it is the first time you do it but it gets easier and more fun with practice. The really hard part is to make the mental adjustment to a new way of thinking.

In conclusion, we might note that it is not absolutely necessary for a utility curve to have a negative side at all. Many companies find it hard even to admit the possibility of a project leading to losses and prefer to assume that all the outcomes are certain thus allowing them to calculate the return on investment. Only those projects having a satisfactory return are then initiated. Most businesses have experience of making losses and there is certainly enough evidence to make the assumption of complete certainty in the project far more 'theoretical' than anything in decision theory. The advantage of the decision theory approach is that it incorporates both probability and loss with the arithmetic becoming trivial once one gets used to it. The trouble is arriving at sensible probabilities in the first place though this is, in reality, no more difficult than any other part of the estimating process. Certainly if we agree that experience forces us to admit the existence of uncertainty in business life then we must surely take account of it in our decision analysis. Probability theory and utility offer an approach to doing this.

Problems

1. Accepting Fig. 5.3 as your utility curve rework the first part of Problem 4 in Chapter 1, assuming the figures to be in thousands of pounds.

2. Making the same assumptions as in Problem 1 of this chapter, rework Problems 1 and 4 of Chapter 3.

3. The management of the Heath Robinson Engineering Company operate a business in which pay offs range from $-£400\,000$ to $+£400\,000$ and they have hired an expert in decision theory to construct their utility curve. The expert decides that £400000 shall be equivalent to 3 U and proceeds to ask a series of questions about the willingness of the company to engage in various projects. He obtains the following information:

Pay offs (£)		Probability required for the larger pay off before HR would be indifferent about the project
−400000	400000	0·625
−200000	400000	0·400
−200000	200000	0·67

Using this information can you infer the Heath Robinson Engineering Company's utility curve?

4. Having looked at the results of the calculation discussed in Problem 3 Heath Robinson now decide that the range should have been from £100000 to £400000 and that £400000 should be equated to 20 U (it hasn't dawned on them that it doesn't matter what value you use to start the curve off and that it is the *shape* of the utility curve that is important). The expert starts again and finds the probabilities and pay offs to be:

Pay offs (£)		Probability required for the larger pay off before HR would be indifferent about the project
−100000	400000	0·78
− 50000	400000	0·50
−100000	100000	0·875
−100000	200000	0·825
− 50000	300000	0·535

Find the utility curve and comment on its shape.

5. The reader is right if he thinks that the answer to the last question was a little too neat to be true. Having learned from Problem 3 how to do the arithmetic he should now try the difficult part of drawing his own utility curve. There is, of course, no solution given but the reader should think about the implications, in his own business, of what he has done.

6

Modifying probabilities by Bayes' theorem

6.1 Prior and posterior probabilities

It very frequently happens that we make a forecast of probabilities in advance of a sequence of events and then are able to revise our assessment as the earlier events unfold.

An example of this is in weather forecasting. The Meteorological Office makes an initial assessment of the following day's weather early in the morning. During the day they receive further information from ships, aircraft, and weather stations and this is used to revise the forecast as the day proceeds. The end result is that the forecast of Tuesday's weather made at 6.00 p.m. on Monday may be quite different from that which was made at 6.00 a.m. on Monday and both of these may well be very different from what actually happens on Tuesday.

Despite the air of confidence with which the forecast is broadcast, it is in fact couched in terms of probabilities. Thus, the forecast made of Tuesday's weather at 6 a.m. on Monday might be—rain 60%, fair 40%. As the day proceeds information is received stating that there is heavy rain in Ireland and the wind is blowing the rain towards England. The wind may change or the rain may stop before the clouds reach England, therefore at 6 p.m. on Monday the forecast for Tuesday might be changed to—rain 80%, fair 20%. In this way the probabilities are being revised from their initial values as other, but still uncertain, information is obtained.

An initial probability statement is called a **prior** probability distribution and one which has been revised in the light of information which has come to hand is called a **posterior** probability distribution. The word **distribution** is used to indicate that the total probability of 1·00 is spread or distributed over a number of collectively exhaustive and mutually exclusive events. It is usual to simplify the terminology to prior distribution and posterior distribution or even merely to prior and posterior. It will be evident that what is a posterior to one sequence of events becomes the prior to others which are yet to happen.

This chapter will be concerned with methods for computing posteriors from priors using a mathematical formula called **Bayes' theorem**, named after the man whose name is given to Bayes' strategies (Chapter 3). Before examining Bayes' theorem in detail we shall first look at an example of the process we call **prior–posterior analysis**.

6.2 The Heath Robinson Engineering Company revisited

The Heath Robinson Engineering Company receives its supplies of a certain component from two suppliers A and B. The proportions are 40% from A and 60% from B.

Supplier A is the more reliable as only about 10% of the batches he supplies are defective. Unfortunately, his capacity is limited and the bulk of the Heath Robinson Engineering Company's requirements have to come from supplier B, 20% of whose batches are faulty. (The figures are chosen for convenience as obviously only the Heath Robinson Engineering Company would put up with such a situation.)

A new batch has just been received which is faulty and the Heath Robinson Engineering Company have decided to complain but unfortunately the store-man cannot remember who supplied it, the documents have been lost, and the goods are unmarked by their maker. Although the Heath Robinson Engineering Company's Managing Director would be far better employed putting right some of the defects in his company he decides to use Bayes' theorem to find the probability that the batch was supplied by company B.

He reasons that 60% of their consumption comes from B and 20% of that is defective. Now, 20% of 60% is 12% so that 12% of what the Heath Robinson Engineering Company buys is defective and comes from B. By the same argument, 40% of the total is from A and 10% of that is faulty so that 10% of 40% (i.e., 4%) is defective and supplied by A. The Heath Robinson Engineering Company's total consumption now breaks down as follows expressed in terms of 100 batches received:

Supplier	Good	Faulty	Total
B	48	12	60
A	36	4	40
Total	84	16	100

Out of every 100 batches supplied, 16 (or 16%) are defective and of these 16, on average, 12 came from B and 4 from A. Thus, the probability that a batch came from B given that it was defective (event D) is a conditional probability, denoted by $P(B|D)$, and calculated from

$$P(B|D) = \frac{12}{16} = 0.75$$

This means there is a 75% chance that a defective batch came from supplier B.

The same result can be achieved by working in probabilities rather than numbers out of 100 batches. The calculation comes down to

$$P(B|D) = \frac{0.20 \times 0.60}{0.20 \times 0.60 + 0.10 \times 0.40}$$

$$= \frac{0.12}{.12 + 0.04} = \frac{0.12}{00.16} = 0.75 \tag{6.1}$$

The top line in this fraction is the same calculation, worked in decimals, as the one which gave the 12 in the middle of the top row in the table, the $0·10 \times 0·40$ is equivalent to the 4 in the middle of the middle row, and so the bottom line of the fraction is equivalent to adding up the middle column of the table to get the 16 in the bottom row.

If the reader has understood the argument which led to the table and the means by which the fraction in Eqn (6.1) was equated to the table, then he has grasped the fundamental principles of Bayes' theorem.

To conclude the Heath Robinson Engineering Company's problem, the Managing Director has decided there is a 75% chance that the batch came from B and, as it must have come from somewhere, there has to be a 25% chance that the batch came from A. This he confirms by using the notation:

A means 'the batch came from A'

D means 'it was defective'

$|$ means 'given that'

Using reasoning like that which led to Eqn (6.1) he writes

$$P(A|D) = \frac{0·10 \times 0·40}{0·10 \times 0·40 + 0·20 \times 0·60}$$

$$= \frac{0·04}{0·04 + 0·12} = \frac{0·04}{0·16} = 0·25$$

Now, the interesting part of this result is that, if the Managing Director had simply been shown the unmarked batch, *without knowing that it was defective*, he would have reasoned thus. 'On average, 60% of our batches come from B so there is a 60% probability that a batch chosen at random came from B and, therefore, a 40% probability that it came from A.' If we use $P(A)$ to denote the probability that a batch comes from A and $P(B)$ that a batch comes from B then, *prior* to getting the information that the batch was defective, the Managing Director would have to write down

$$P(A) = 0·40$$

and

$$P(B) = 0·60$$

This statement shows how the probabilities were distributed originally and is therefore called the **prior distribution**.

After getting the information about the defectiveness of the batch the Managing Director can make a revised or posterior statement about the probabilities. Let us write $P^*(A)$ and $P^*(B)$ to indicate the probabilities that this batch came from A and B respectively, *after* including the knowledge that it was faulty. The Managing Director can now make the posterior-probability statement

$$P^*(A) = 0·25$$
$$P^*(B) = 0·75$$

and this is the **posterior distribution.**

In this case, he might well decide that as there is only a 75% chance of being right if he complains to B, he might be shown up if they can prove they didn't supply it. He had better spend his time making sure that documents don't get lost again and in looking for more quality-conscious suppliers.

Having explored the woes of the Heath Robinson Engineering Company for illustrative purposes we can now discuss Bayes' theorem in more detail.

6.3 Bayes' theorem

The theory of probability leads, very simply, to Bayes' theorem which we have seen to be of some use in deriving probabilities. Despite its usefulness it was unused for about 200 years following its discovery, mainly because it was used by Laplace, one of the greatest mathematicians of all time, to prove that there was rather a low probability that the Sun would rise tomorrow. As the Sun continued to rise, apparently in defiance of the laws of mathematics, it was thought that Bayes was wrong. This was rather hard as it overlooked the fact that Laplace had, perhaps humorously, used the formula wrongly. Eventually, it transpired that nothing was wrong with the Sun, Bayes' theorem, or the laws of mathematics, the latter being of great relief to mathematicians with visions of unemployment. The result was that Bayes' theorem could be resurrected for the benefit of modern businessmen.*

The theorem is a means of deriving probabilities, linking effects with their possible causes. Suppose that there are two causes, C_1 and C_2, and two possible effects which can be observed, E_1 and E_2. In Section 6.2 the causes were

C_1 batch made by A

and

C_2 batch made by B

and the effects were

E_1 batch is faulty
E_2 batch is satisfactory

We have to know the probabilities of the two causes, $P(C_1)$ and $P(C_2)$, just as we knew $P(A)$ and $P(B)$ to be the prior probabilities that a batch chosen at random came from A and B. We also have to know the conditional probabilities, that a particular cause would lead to a specified effect. These are written as $P(E_1|C_1)$ and $P(E_1|C_2)$ where the vertical line means 'given that'.

Bayes' theorem states, for example, that,

$$P(C_1|E_1) = \frac{P(E_1|C_1)P(C_1)}{P(E_1|C_1)P(C_1) + P(E_1|C_2)P(C_2)} \qquad (6.2)$$

* The proof of Bayes' Theorem is interesting mainly to mathematicians and need not be given here. The reader who followed Section 6.2 should manage the rest of the chapter. For the proof see my *Mathematics for Business Decisions*, Nelson, London, 1971, p. 223.

Equation (6.2) is called **Bayes' formula**. We can also write an identical formula for $P(C_2|E_1)$ and that is

$$P(C_2|E_1) = \frac{P(E_1|C_2)P(C_2)}{P(E_1|C_2)P(C_2) + P(E_1|C_1)P(C_1)} \qquad (6.3)$$

We now apply Eqns (6.2) and (6.3) to the problem of the Heath Robinson Engineering Company to check that they give the same results as we previously obtained by logical argument.

For the Heath Robinson Engineering Company we had

$$P(C_1) = 0\cdot40$$
$$P(C_2) = 0\cdot60$$
$$P(E_1|C_1) = 0\cdot10$$
$$P(E_1|C_2) = 0\cdot20$$

recalling the statement above linking C_1 with A, C_2 with B, and E_1 with D. Substituting directly into Eqn (6.2) we have

$$P(C_1|E_1) = \frac{0\cdot10 \times 0\cdot40}{0\cdot10 \times 0\cdot40 + 0\cdot20 \times 0\cdot60}$$

$$= \frac{0\cdot04}{0\cdot16}$$

$$= 0\cdot25$$

and in Eqn (6.3) we get

$$P(C_2|E_1) = \frac{0\cdot20 \times 0\cdot60}{0\cdot20 \times 0\cdot60 + 0\cdot10 \times 0\cdot40}$$

$$= \frac{0\cdot12}{0\cdot16}$$

$$= 0\cdot75$$

These are the results we had before so we can insert * to denote the posterior distribution of C_1 and C_2 and write

$$P^*(C_1) = P(C_1|E_1) = 0\cdot25$$
$$P^*(C_2) = P(C_2|E_2) = 0\cdot75$$

At this point the reader may find it helpful to pause and compare the calculations we have just done with those in Section 6.2 and to match Eqns (6.2) and (6.3) with his logical understanding of the calculations which led to, and followed, the table in Section 6.2.

In looking at the equations it may be helpful to notice that the top line of the fraction is repeated at the beginning of the bottom line. The rest of the bottom line is the same as the top line except that the identifying number (technically known as a **subscript**) is changed to the other possibility. The conditional probabilities on the right-hand side of the equation have the same subscripts for E and C as the probability we are trying to find, but the order of the symbols is reversed. The posterior probability we are trying to find is a conditional probability because it gives the probability for C on condition that a particular E has been observed.

6.4 Further details about Bayes' formula

What happens if we observe not E_1 but E_2? The formulae can be written out in much the same way as before, being careful to get the identifying numbers on the E's and C's in the right combination. The reader should perhaps try it himself before looking at the answer, which is overleaf.

$$P(C_1|E_2)=\frac{P(E_2|C_1)P(C_1)}{P(E_2|C_1)P(C_1)+P(E_2|C_2)P(C_2)}$$

and

$$P(C_2|E_2)=\frac{P(E_2|C_2)P(C_2)}{P(E_2|C_2)P(C_2)+P(E_2|C_1)P(C_1)}$$

6.5 Another example of Bayes' theorem

For a further illustration, suppose that the batch in the Heath Robinson Engineering Company's problem had been satisfactory. What are the probabilities that it came from suppliers A and B?

We use the same relationship between E's and C's and A, B and D which were used in Section 6.3 and we now need to find

$$P(C_1|E_2) \quad \text{and} \quad P(C_2|E_2)$$

for which we have formulae but not all of the probabilities. We can, however, proceed by making use of the fact that there is an important limitation on the validity of Bayes' theorem. This is, that the collection of E's and the collection of C's must each form a collectively exhaustive and mutually exclusive group. In this case they do, so we exploit the requirement which follows from collective exhaustivity and mutual exclusion which is that

$$P(E_1|C_1)+P(E_2|C_1)=1\cdot00$$

In words—*for a given cause the probabilities of the collectively exhaustive and mutually exclusive effects must add up to 1·00 as they must always do for any collectively exhaustive and mutually exclusive grouping of any kind of event.*

As we know that $P(E_1|C_1)=0\cdot10$ and $P(E_1|C_2)=0\cdot20$, we can find $P(E_2|C_1)$ and $P(E_2|C_2)$, then calculate $P(C_1|E_2)$ and $P(C_2|E_2)$ to find

$$P(C_1|E_2)=0\cdot43$$
$$P(C_2|E_2)=0\cdot57$$

The reader should check these figures.

Again, we can compare these posterior values with the prior distribution for C_1 and C_2 which was $P(C_1)=0\cdot40$ and $P(C_2)=0\cdot60$.

There is much less difference here between the posterior and the prior than there was in the case where the batch was defective. This is because defective batches are a good deal less common than satisfactory ones, therefore the information that a batch is defective is fairly rare and thus more significant. We should expect significant information to make a fairly large change in an outlook, relative to that made by common information, and this is precisely what happens.

This can be seen even more strongly if we take $P(E_1|C_1)=0.01$ and $P(E_1|C_2)=0.02$. (The reader should make sure he understands what these are.) We now get

$$P(C_1|E_1)=0.25$$
$$P(C_2|E_1)=0.75$$

as before, but

$$P(C_1|E_2)=0.403$$
$$P(C_2|E_2)=0.597$$

The relative change from prior to posterior in the two cases is now even more striking when compared with $P(C_1)=0.40$ and $P(C_2)=0.60$.

This illustrates the remarkable information–converting power of Bayes' theorem. We shall now generalize the theorem to more complex cases and then we shall deal with such a problem.

6.6 The general form of the theorem

Bayes' formula is of perfectly general application regardless of the numbers of causes and effects in the problem. For example, if there are two effects and three causes and E_1 has been observed, the posterior probability for the first cause would be

$$P(C_1|E_1)=\frac{P(E_1|C_1)P(C_1)}{P(E_1|C_1)P(C_1)+P(E_1|C_2)P(C_2)+P(E_1|C_3)P(C_3)}$$

The top line in this formula is the same as in Eqn (6.2) and the bottom line is also the same, except for the addition of the conditional probability for the first effect and the third cause, multiplied by the prior probability for the third cause.

This result can be extended to any number of causes by extending the bottom line in the equation by adding on similar items.

It is very easy to write a computer program to do this calculation for any number of causes and effects, indeed this is to be recommended in practice. It saves an awful lot of arithmetic and, if the programmer pays some attention to the layout of the results, the computer analysis is very easy to interpret and extremely useful in practice.

6.7 A more complicated example

The case we have used to illustrate the calculations was simple and the numbers were easy to manipulate but it does not have the flavour of a real problem. We now examine a more complex problem which, though still simplified, shows more clearly how Bayes' theorem allows one to incorporate information into an analysis and how widely divergent initial views come closer together, as they should, in the light of factual information.

Mass Marketing Ltd has resolved to launch yet another new product, a health food, on an unsuspecting public. The product will be sold through several thousand retail chemists but advertising will be handled centrally by Mass Marketing Ltd. There will be an advertising campaign every month, for the first 4 months, and in each campaign the public will be invited to contact one of Mass Marketing Ltd's Regional Offices for advice about the product and the names of local dealers. The number of these contacts will have to serve as an indication of the way things are going because the distribution chain is so long and the retailers are so bad at providing information that it will be several months before Mass Marketing Ltd know how the product has sold. There is no guarantee that potential customers, to whom information is sent, will in fact buy the product and there is nothing to stop a purchaser buying it without contacting Mass Marketing Ltd first. However, Mass Marketing Ltd have had experience of this kind of promotion in the past and they know that when sales have actually been bad, indifferent, and good then the probability of having requests for information at the various levels is:

		Requests were		
		Low (L)	Medium (M)	High (H)
	bad (B)	0·80	0·10	0·10
Sales were	indifferent (I)	0·20	0·60	0·20
	good (G)	0·10	0·30	0·60

These probabilities add to 1·0 across the rows, as they ought, but not down the columns since there is no reason why they should.

So far so good. The information in the table is based on reasonably sound factual data and Mass Marketing Ltd feel that the present circumstances compare quite well with past experience so the principle of repeatability applies and it is valid to use the historical table in this new situation.

There are three directors of the firm and they are quite unable to agree on their assessment regarding the probabilities of the eventual outcome for this particular promotion. One director has no strong views and is denoted by N (Neutral), and thinks that $P_N(B)=0·3$, $P_N(I)=0·4$, and $P_N(G)=0·3$. The N denotes that these are his views and the probabilities express his view that the three outcomes are more or less equally likely. His co-directors, Optimist and Pessimist, are fairly adamant that

$$P_O(B)=0·1 \qquad P_P(B)=0·7$$
$$P_O(I)=0·2 \qquad P_P(I)=0·2$$
$$P_O(G)=0·7 \qquad P_P(G)=0·1$$

These are almost diametrically opposed views.

The scheme is implemented and, in the first 3 months, the requests for information are continuously high. Now, this is obviously information of some value and the Directors should really take it into account in their views of the probabilities regarding the eventual outcomes of the project. On the other hand, their initial probability statements reflect their separate experience, wisdom, and judgement and, although they are obviously not all right, they cannot be expected to reject all their previous experience just for 3 months' data from one project. We shall now see how Bayes' theorem enables us to merge the prior probabilities with the information available, month by month, and how the three initial views converge towards a common point. First, we consider the case of Pessimist. His prior distribution was

$$P_P(B) = 0.7$$
$$P_P(I) = 0.2$$
$$P_P(G) = 0.1$$

and he has the same performance results from previous advertising campaigns, namely:

		Enquiries		
		L	M	H
	B	0·80	0·10	0·10
Sales	I	0·20	0·60	0·20
	G	0·10	0·30	0·60

He reasons that, if sales are going to be bad there is an 80% chance of low enquiries, 10% of medium enquiries, and 10% of high enquiries. He has already said that he thinks there is a 70% chance of sales being bad so there should be a 0.70×0.80 probability that sales will be bad *and* enquiries will be low, a 0.70×0.10 probability that sales will be bad and enquiries will be medium, and a 0.70×0.10 probability that sales will be bad and enquiries will be high. These are **joint** probabilities and calculations of this sort were discussed in Chapter 2. The values are found by taking the prior probability of 0·70 and using it to multiply each entry in the first row of the data table. Similarly, we can take the 0·20 which is Pessimist's probability of indifferent sales and multiply the second row in the data table, and the 10% probability of good sales and multiply the third row. We get:

Joint probability table

		Enquiries		
		L	M	H
	B	0·56	0·07	0·07
Sales	I	0·04	0·12	0·04
	G	0·01	0·03	0·06
		─────	────	────
Total		0·61	0·22	0·17

The grand total of 0·61, 0·22, and 0·17 is 1·00. Now, this is what the grand total should be because it expresses the probabilities which Pessimist would assign to each of the nine combinations of enquiries and sales with his prior distribution and the conditional probability table.

The figure of 0·56 is, for example,

$$P(L|B)P(B)$$

and the total of 0·61 is

$$P(L|B)P(B) + P(L|I)P(I) + P(L|G)P(G)$$

The rest of the table has a similar interpretation. In particular, the three column totals are Pessimist's assessment of the probabilities of low, medium, and high enquiries.

Now, at the end of the first month, these probabilities became rather academic as the level of enquiries was high during the month. This is factual information about what enquiries actually were and there is no longer any point in talking about the probabilities of getting medium or low enquiries in the first month. The value of 0·17, assigned by Pessimist at the beginning of the month to the probability of high, now has to be altered to 1·00 to allow for the *fact* of high, which becomes known at the end of the month. However, a high level of enquiries could arise when the underlying market is bad, indifferent, and good so that we now have to calculate P_P*—Pessimist's posterior distribution for the three states of the market at the end of the first month. This is, of course, the standard Bayesian calculation which we did intuitively in Section 6.2, the answer being

$$P_P*^1(B) = \frac{0·07}{0·17} = 0·41$$

$$P_P*^1(I) = \frac{0·04}{0·17} = 0·24$$

$$P_P*^1(G) = \frac{0·06}{0·17} = 0·35$$

and these three values add to 1·00 which they should. The superscript 1 denotes one piece of information. The reader will notice the change from the original prior which was 0·7, 0·2, and 0·1, respectively.

The calculation we have just done could be performed equally well by using one of the forms of Bayes' formula. For example,

$$P(B|H) = \frac{P(H|B)P(B)}{P(H|B)P(B) + P(H|I)P(I) + P(H|G)P(G)}$$

$$= \frac{0·10 \times 0·70}{0·10 \times 0·70 + 0·20 \times 0·20 + 0·60 \times 0·10}$$

$$= \frac{0·07}{0·07 + 0·04 + 0·06}$$

$$= \frac{0·07}{0·16}$$

$$= 0·41$$

as before, and similarly for the other probabilities.

Mass Marketing Ltd has now reached the start of month 2 in which the enquiries will again be high, though they don't know that. Unless Pessimist is prepared to reject the first month's evidence completely he will have to take, as his new prior distribution, the posterior he has just calculated. This is reasonable because 1 month's evidence is hardly conclusive and the values he has got are 0·41, 0·24, and 0·35 which indicate no very clear view on the subject. He still regards a bad market as the most likely outcome but is now thinking rather more positively about the possibilities of indifferent or good. Given his initial views and the small amount of evidence available from month 1 this seems a reasonable view.

At the start of month 2, Pessimist calculates a new joint probability table by using his new prior values to multiply each of the entries in the corresponding row of the data or conditional probability table, which remains unchanged by 1 month's data.

He gets:

Month 2 start

Enquiries

		New prior	Conditional			Joint		
			L	*M*	*H*	*L*	*M*	*H*
	B	0·41	0·80	0·10	0·10	0·33	0·04	0·04
Market	I	0·24	0·20	0·60	0·20	0·05	0·14	0·05
	G	0·35	0·10	0·30	0·60	0·04	0·10	0·21
			Total			0·42	0·28	0·30

We can deduce from the totals of the joint probability table that Pessimist has a higher expectation (42%) of there being low enquiries this month than any other outcome, with nearly equal probabilities for medium and high enquiries—28% and 30% respectively.

Now, at the end of month 2 the fact is that enquiries have again been high. Pessimist now calculates a new posterior with a superscript of 2 to show that it now incorporates 2 months' results. He gets

$$P_P^{*2}(B) = \frac{0·04}{0·30} = 0·13$$

$$P_P^{*2}(I) = \frac{0·05}{0·30} = 0·17$$

$$P_P^{*2}(G) = \frac{0·21}{0·30} = 0·70$$

His view has now changed very considerably and he moves into the third month by calculating a new joint table using this distribution as his prior. He calculates:

Month 3 start

Enquiries

		New prior	Conditional			Joint		
			L	M	H	L	M	H
	B	0·13	0·80	0·10	0·10	0·104	0·013	0·013
Market	I	0·17	0·20	0·60	0·25	0·034	0·102	0·034
	G	0·70	0·110	0·30	0·60	0·070	0·210	0·420
			Total			0·208	0·325	0·467

Three places of decimals have now appeared in the joint table. This is simply a device to ensure that the totals add to 1·00. In calculations like this there is always a risk that serious error can creep in through an accumulation of small distortions in the figures, caused by rounding-off to two decimal places. To avoid these errors it may be necessary to carry one extra decimal place in the calculation, and this is what we have done. The reader should be cautioned that the results have not become more precise. The original prior has probably only an accuracy of one decimal place and the final answer will be no better than that.

At the end of the third month the level of enquiries is again found to have been high and Pessimist now calculates his final posterior, giving it a super-script of 3 to show that it is the result of 3 months' experience. His result is

$$P_P*^3(B) = \frac{0·013}{0·467} = 0·03$$

$$P_P*^3(I) = \frac{0·034}{0·467} = 0·07$$

$$P_P*^3(G) = \frac{0·420}{0·467} = 0·90$$

This shows a very considerable change from his original view which is as it should be, considering the very clear nature of the evidence.

Having achieved this result how shall we use it?

Mass Marketing Ltd has done pay off calculations of the type shown in Chapter 3 on previous occasions. They know the pay offs from the various market states and the costs of another month's advertising. They decide to review the advertising campaign every month and decide on the basis of expected value whether to continue or terminate the project. In a sense, each month's advertising expenditure is the purchase price of information about the market. In order to solve each month's expected value calculation they need to have probabilities and these are precisely what are furnished by the Bayesian analysis we have just done. We shall not embark on the expected value calculations as they would be exactly the same as the ones we have shown earlier. The only difference is that the probabilities, instead of being only initial estimates, would steadily reflect the change wrought by incorporating the information bought month by month.

Another way of dealing with this problem of a sequence of decision with uncertain outcomes would be to draw up a decision tree, using Bayes' theorem to calculate the revised probabilities following each possible outcome at every stage in the tree. With the aid of a pre-written computer program on a time-sharing system, or half an hour with a slide rule, the calculations are not overly laborious.

We should now complete the Mass Marketing Ltd problem by looking at the case of Optimist and Neutral to see how their probabilities are changed by the sample information. We give the results for Optimist in full, though without explanation, and those for Neutral in summary only. The reader who seeks full understanding, if not a practitioner's competence, should work the calculations for himself.

Optimist's calculations

Month 1 start

Enquiries

		Original prior	*Conditional*			*Joint*		
			L	*M*	*H*	*L*	*M*	*H*
	B	0·10	0·80	0·10	0·10	0·08	0·01	0·01
Market	I	0·20	0·20	0·60	0·20	0·04	0·12	0·04
	G	0·70	0·10	0·30	0·60	0·07	0·21	0·42
			Total			0·19	0·34	0·47

$$Po^{*1}(B) = \frac{0·01}{0·47} = 0·021$$

$$Po^{*1}(I) = \frac{0·04}{0·47} = 0·085$$

$$Po^{*1}(G) = \frac{0·42}{0·47} = 0·894$$

Total 1·000   Check

Month 2 Start

Enquiries

		New prior	*Conditonal*			*Joint*		
			L	*M*	*H*	*L*	*M*	*H*
	B	0·021	0·80	0·10	0·10	0·017	0·002	0·002
Market	I	0·085	0·20	0·60	0·20	0·017	0·051	0·017
	G	0·894	0·10	0·30	0·60	0·089	0·268	0·537
			Total			0·123	0·321	0·556

$$P_O*^2(B)=0.003$$
$$P_O*^2(I)=0.031$$
$$P_O*^2(G)=0.965$$

Total 1·000   Check

Month 3 start

Enquiries

Market		New prior	Conditional L	M	H	Joint L	M	H
	B	0·003	0·80	0·10	0·10	0·002	0·000	0·000
	I	0·031	0·20	0·60	0·20	0·006	0·019	0·006
	G	0·965	0·10	0·30	0·60	0·097	0·290	0·580
			Total			0·105	0·309	0·586

$$P_O*^3(B)=0.00$$
$$P_O*^3(I)=0.01$$
$$P_O*^3(G)=0.99$$

Total 1·00   Check

The entries of 0·000 do not mean zero probability but that the probability has become so small that even three decimal places are not sufficient to measure it.

Neutral's results

Market		Original prior	Posterior after: 1 month	2 months	3 months
	B	0·3	0·10	0·02	0·00
	I	0·4	0·36	0·18	0·07
	G	0·3	0·54	0·80	0·93

To show the convergence of views which has taken place we now summarize with a comparative table for Optimist (O), Pessimist (P), and Neutral (N).

Person		Original prior O	N	P	1 month O	N	P	2 months O	N	P	3 months O	N	P
Market	B	0·1	0·3	0·7	0·02	0·10	0·41	0·00	0·02	0·13	0·00	0·00	0·03
	I	0·2	0·4	0·2	0·08	0·36	0·24	0·03	0·18	0·17	0·01	0·07	0·07
	G	0·7	0·3	0·1	0·90	0·54	0·35	0·97	0·80	0·70	0·99	0·93	0·90

Clearly, there has been a fairly strong convergence of views which is what should have happened with the fairly strong evidence provided by three highs in a row. The remarkable thing is that Bayes' theorem leads to this very marked zeroing-in effect even from such widely divergent starting points. Had the sequence been less clear, say high, low, medium, there would have been much less convergence to a common final posterior as the reader may care to confirm by calculation. Again, that is as it should be because the evidence would then not be clear enough to outweigh the previous convictions of the three individuals.

The core of the result of this chapter is embodied in the extreme left-hand and right-hand blocks of the last table. The left-hand side shows the probability distributions with which O, N, and P started the 3-month time period. The three distributions are about as far apart as they could be. At the right-hand side are their final assessments taking into account the available evidence. The agreement is remarkable. It is important to realize that if P, for example, said that after 3-months' results his probability distribution was *not* 0·03, 0·07, and 0·90, then he is being inconsistent with his earlier judgement of 0·7, 0·2, and 0·1. He cannot now turn round and say that he did not mean 0·7, 0·2, and 0·1 after all but really thought that it was, say, 0·98, 0·01, and 0·01. To do so would very much be acting with hindsight and would certainly call into question the maturity of his original judgement. It was remarked earlier that one of the more disconcerting features of decision theory is that it quite rigorously exposes inconsistency, irrationality, and assumptions to public view. The benefits from this in terms of sheer improved management would be very hard to overstate. Compared with the benefits the labour of the arithmetic is trivial. What is hard, of course, is not understanding and applying the theory but inculcating the appropriate mental attitude.

Problems

1. Three causes, A, B, and C, are linked to three effects, D, E, and F, by probabilities which may be expressed as

		Probability that the effect will be		
		D	E	F
	A	0·7	0·3	0·0
Cause	B	0·2	0·5	0·3
	C	0·1	0·6	0·3

The 'effects' might be that a batch of product is poor (D), satisfactory (E), or good (F). The 'causes' could be that the process was running badly (A), adequately (B), or well (C). The table then says, for example, that if the process is running badly there is a 70% chance that the product will be poor, or 30% chance that it will be satisfactory, and no chance that it will be good.

The probabilities that the process is running badly, adequately, and well are respectively 0·2, 0·6, and 0·2. A batch of product is observed to be poor so what are the revised probabilities for the condition of the process?

2. In problem 1 the company has a policy of adjusting the process at the weekend if it appears to be running badly. Once the decision is made to adjust the process or to leave it alone it cannot be changed until the next weekend. The process produces one batch per week and this batch is tested, partly to provide information on the state of the process. The pay offs involved are

(i) Adjusting the process when it is really running adequately or well – 400
(ii) Adjusting the process when it is running badly 300
(iii) Not adjusting the process when it is really running badly – 300
(iv) Not adjusting when it is really running well 0

In the light of Problem 1 what are the maximum EV actions before and after the information that the batch was poor?

3. Heath Robinson Engineering manufacture fork lift trucks in one of their divisions. The division has several minor competitors, mostly very small, and one major rival. The rival has recently introduced a new type of truck which is selling fairly well as far as HR can tell. HR are trying to decide whether or not to introduce a competing truck and one of the major factors in this decision is the likely action of the rival. HR feel that the rival could expand production of the new truck, keep it about the same level or cut it back. From past experience of what the rival has done and the nature of the market for trucks HR think that the chances of the three actions are respectively 50%, 30%, and 20%. The only information they can get is from a study of the rival's advertisements in the technical press and they have assigned probabilities to the rival reducing, maintaining, and increasing his advertising. They express the probabilities as follows:

| | | *Effects* | | |
| | | *Advertising will be* | | |
		I *Reduced*	II *Maintained*	III *Increased*
	A Cut back	0·60	0·30	0·10
Cause	B Keep at the	0·40	0·40	0·20
Rival is going to	same level			
	C Expand	0·20	0·30	0·50

They observe that, during the following month, advertising is increased. What are HR's revised probabilities for the rival's course of action?

4. Most of this chapter is a problem and the reader who wants to understand Bayes' theorem would do well to go through the whole thing again.

5. Having really mastered the example in the chapter the reader should rework it on the basis that the level of enquiries was high, low, high, in the three successive months.

7

The economics of information

7.1 The basic ideas

So far in the book we have been looking at problems in which there were alternative actions each of which led to uncertain outcomes. We could attach pay offs or opportunity losses to any particular combination of action and outcome. Precisely because the outcomes were uncertain we dealt first with rather defensive methods of choosing actions, for example maximin pay off and minimax opportunity loss. Having decided that these methods were not always satisfactory we then changed to expected monetary value or expected utility and chose actions which would maximize whichever of these measures we decided to use. In order to use the measure at all we had to be able to attach probabilities to the outcomes and we have spent many pages on calculations involving probabilities.

The fundamental weakness of all these methods is that they still do not tell us what is going to happen. We are forced to admit that we are facing an uncertain future and, though we have ideas, which we express as probability distributions, about the likelihood of what *might* happen, we absolutely do not know what *will* happen. We try to hedge our bets by using the idea of repeatability and relying, in effect, on recouping on the swings what we lose on the roundabouts. In fact, we take this idea one stage further by using very large negative utilities for losses and by not embarking on a project at all if its expected utility is negative. In this way we ensure that, in the reasonably long run, the 'swings' will more than pay for the 'roundabouts' so that we shall have an attractively profitable business.

However, even with all these precautions and refinements we still have to live in an economic world where the unexpected can and does happen so there is always the chance that we shall make losses if things go badly or even that we shall do less well than we otherwise might have had we known in advance what the outcome was to be.

It would, in fact, be rather convenient if, when faced with a choice of actions each of which led to an uncertain outcome, we could retain the services of a consultant Good Fairy to tell us what the future held in store. Armed with that information we should then take the correct action and the opportunity loss would be zero. This would obviously be a big improvement over the situation in Chapter 3 where we were forced to choose the action which led to the smallest expected opportunity loss. In effect, perfect information of the type promised by good fairies has a value equal to the opportunity losses we can avoid by having it. It may, of course, also have a price and we should have to try to decide whether the information would be worth buying without knowing what it would be. Deciding questions like this is what the **economics of information** is about.

It is unfortunately true that good fairies are seldom found on the staffs of modern corporations, or indeed among consultants. Even if they were, we would have to bear in mind that the Delphic Oracle in Ancient Greece had a distressing habit of making rather vague pronouncements which could always be misinterpreted, thus rendering the information less than perfect. Now-adays, we have available to us a whole battery of methods such as statistical analysis, market research, and opinion polling. Despite the sophistication of their methods and equipment and the skill and competence of their staffs the fact has to be faced that they do not always get the right answer, as politicians and companies have found to their cost. Perhaps this is because the data they have is inadequate or because the very fact of asking questions about a subject under study distorts the views people hold. Whatever the reason, however, the information provided by these **sample surveys**, as they are called, is not perfect. Nonetheless, as well as a price, sample information does have some value, because it often is correct.

Clearly, in order to be complete, the theory of economics of information must include both the value of perfect information (VPI) and the value of sample information (VSI). The theory must also take account of uncertainty because we have to commit ourselves to paying for the information before we know what it is to be. We therefore speak of the **expected value of perfect information** (EVPI) and the **expected value of sample informa-tion** (EVSI). We shall now examine some of this theory.

In what follows we shall work exclusively with pay off and opportunity loss tables. The calculations could equally well be performed with utility, pro-viding one had a suitable conversion chart. In many cases this would be preferable, for the reasons examined in Chapter 5. As such a curve reflects the particular values of a decision-maker it is a personal preference and, in order to keep the explanations unencumbered with arbitrary utility values we shall keep to £ or monetary units (m.u.) rather than utility (U).

7.2 The expected value of perfect information

Consider a simple decision problem with actions A, B, and C, outcomes I, II, and III, and pay offs in monetary units, of

Pay off table

		Outcome		
		I	II	III
	A	150	40	10
Action	B	90	160	110
	C	60	120	190

We immediately convert the pay offs into opportunity losses to get the conditional opportunity loss table:

COL table

		Outcome I	II	III
	A	0	120	180
Action	B	60	0	80
	C	90	40	0

(The reader may find it useful to review Chapter 1 in order to refresh his memory about this step.)

If probabilities are assigned to outcomes I, II, and III of 0·5, 0·2, and 0·3 respectively, we would calculate, as in Chapter 3, the expected opportunity losses of A, B, and C getting

$$EOL(A) = 0·5 \times 0 + 0·2 \times 120 + 0·3 \times 180 = 78$$
$$EOL(B) = 0·5 \times 60 + 0·2 \times 0 + 0·3 \times 80 = 54$$
$$EOL(C) = 0·5 \times 90 + 0·2 \times 40 + 0·3 \times 0 = 53$$

From these three values we see that C has the lowest EOL and this would be the optimal action. The EOL would then be 53 m.u.

Now, if we knew for certain in advance of the decision that the outcome was going to be I the optimal action would be A with an opportunity loss of 0. If we had perfect information that the outcome was to be II we should choose action B, again with an OL of 0 and, if we were guaranteed that the outcome would be III the optimal action would be C and again the OL would then be 0. Thus, it is clear that if we were to be given *perfectly accurate* information about what the outcome was going to be we could always choose an action leading to a zero opportunity loss. However, if we are not to be given that information we have to select action C and make do with an expected opportunity loss of 53 m.u. Thus, the *expected* value of the perfect information would be 53 m.u. because that is the opportunity loss we can avoid by getting it. Since this value of 53 involves probabilities we must treat it as an expected value.

We have to point out, of course, that the opportunity loss will not be 53 at all. It will be 0, 40, or 90 according to the outcome being III, II, or I, respectively. We have to rely again on the ideas of repeatability, which were discussed earlier, and say that we assume that in a reasonable number of similar projects we could average an OL of 53 per project by choosing C. This kind of hidden assumption crops up fairly regularly in decision theory and each case has to be checked on its merits to make sure that the assumption is reasonably justified.

It is one of the several advantages of the opportunity loss measure that the EVPI is always identical to the minimum expected opportunity loss.

7.3 EVPI—another example

Consider a problem in which there are, as in the previous example, three actions and three outcomes. The pay off table is very nearly the same as in the last problem, only the bottom row has been changed, and the probabilities are the same. The pay off table is:

Pay off table

		Outcome		
		I	II	III
	A	150	40	10
Action	B	90	160	110
	C	120	120	90

The conditional opportunity loss table and the expected opportunity losses are:

COL table

		Outcome			
		I	II	III	EOL
Probability		0·5	0·2	0·3	
	A	0	120	100	54
Action	B	60	0	0	30
	C	30	40	20	29

The EVPI is found by observing that if we are told that the outcome is to be I we shall choose action A whereas if it is II or III we should select action B. In either case we get a zero opportunity loss as opposed to the minimum EOL of 29 so once again the EVPI is the same as the minimum EOL which is 29 in this case.

It is rather interesting that this example says that with a criterion of minimizing EOL we should choose action C whereas if we had perfect information the choice would never fall on C. This is purely because of the way the problem has been constructed but it illustrates the rather curious things which can arise in decision theory. The explanation in this case is that action C is a more consistent performer than A or B. However, for any particular outcome, either A or B will be rather better than C but the other one will be very much worse, particularly outcomes II and III. It follows, fairly naturally, that knowing what the outcome was going to be, we would *never* choose C but without that information we would choose it because of its consistency. Again, common sense and decision theory confirm one another in a simple case. The theory really comes into its own in situations which are so complex that common sense is unable to cope. The calculations would be exactly the same only longer.

7.4 Using EVPI

In the example of Section 7.2 we concluded by saying that the EVPI was 53 m.u. How should we use that result?

Let us suppose that the example refers to the Heath Robinson Engineering Company who have the choice of building three designs of aircraft-handling equipment which we refer to as A, B, and C. There are three new types of aircraft under development (I, II, and III) and the Heath Robinson Engineering Company's pay off depends on which of these is bought by a particularly important airline.

This airline has already made its choice of aircraft and offers to tell the Heath Robinson Engineering Company in confidence what their choice is, in return for a reduction in the price of machines sold by the company to them. The Heath Robinson Engineering Company knows that the type of aircraft chosen by this airline will inevitably be adopted by many other smaller airlines. Therefore, advance information like this would be commercially valuable as the Heath Robinson Engineering Company could ensure that they had the right equipment available at the right time. These values have been expressed in the pay off table so that, as we have seen, the EVPI would be 53 m.u. The theory regarding the economics of information states that the Heath Robinson Engineering Company should be prepared to pay (by way of a cut-price deal to the major airline) *no more than the EVPI* for the information.

This is, in fact, rather a superficial view of the theory because the purchase of the information is an investment in itself and therefore should show a return. Alternatively, it could be argued that the information is a kind of wholesale commodity which will be converted into retail by being used to help market the right products. On this view there should be some kind of mark-up between the purchase price of the information and the EVPI.

Yet another view is that there just is no such thing as perfect information and there is always room for error, second thoughts, or simply accidents.

On all these views the purchase price should be less than the EVPI and a rough rule of thumb is that the purchase price should not be more than half the EVPI. Obviously, this is going to depend on the circumstances.

7.5 The expected value of sample information

At the last minute, before any cash or information has changed hands, the airline changes its mind and withdraws from the whole deal for reasons they will not disclose.

This leaves the Heath Robinson Engineering Company in a bit of a fix because they would still like to forecast which of the three aircraft models (I, II, or III) is going to come into service so that they can decide which machine (A, B, or C) to develop. They decide to approach a leading aviation expert to ask him to forecast which of I, II, or III it will be. He says that his fee for the study will be 20 m.u. (which is a lot of money) and the Heath Robinson Engineering Company have to decide whether to retain his services or not. This expert has many years of experience of the industry and has very good information available to him. He writes in one of the newspapers about aviation affairs and, by studying back-copies of the paper, the Heath Robinson Engineering Company decide that his forecasts are correct about 90% of the time. In effect this means that, if they retain his consulting services, he will study the problem and present a report saying, very nicely, that, for example, 'the airlines are going to adopt model 2', and there will be a 90% chance that he will be proved right when the airlines do place their orders. Whatever he says, the Heath Robinson Engineering Company can tell from the opportunity loss table what they should do, their problem now is should they pay him to say it? In short, what is the expected value of his forecast? As the forecast is not guaranteed to be correct, it is called a sample, and the value we are looking for is the expected value of sample information or EVSI. How do we calculate it?

The method is to calculate the expected opportunity loss as though the information was available, which we denote by EOLI, and compare this with the original minimum EOL. The difference between the two values is the reduction in EOL which would be brought about by the information and this will be the expected value of sample information. This is precisely equivalent to the method used in finding EVPI. It will be recalled that the EVPI, because it is for *perfect* information, reduces the minimum EOL to zero and we had

$$EVPI = minimum\ EOL$$

and this is the same as saying

$$EVPI = minimum\ EOL - zero$$

For EVSI we say

$$EVSI = minimum\ EOL - EOLI$$

For the present problem we proceed as follows. The old COL table from Section 7.2 was, with the probabilities written in for convenience,

COL table

		Outcome		
		I	II	III
Probability		0·5	0·2	0·3
	A	0	120	180
Action	B	60	0	80
	C	90	40	0

We now simply work through the possible reports the consultant *could* make calculating in each case a new optimal act and thereby working out what the EOLI's would be.

Suppose, the consultant forecasts outcome I. We know that there is a 90% chance of him being right and therefore a 10% probability of his being wrong. In the absence of any further information we have to assume that if he is wrong it is equally likely that the outcome will be II or III if he has said it will be I. This means that, if he says it will be outcome I there will be a new probability distribution of 0·9, 0·05, and 0·05 for outcomes I, II, and III, respectively. This is all the information we need to work out a perfectly standard EOL calculation to find EOLI (I), which is the EOL for the optimal act with the information that the consultant has forecast outcome I. Notice, that we cannot automatically assume that the Heath Robinson Engineering Company should take action A when the consultant forecasts outcome I because of the probability that he will be wrong and the large opportunity losses which could arise if he was.

Applying the usual EOL calculation we get:

COL table for forecast of outcome

		Outcome			
		I	II	III	EOL
New probability		0·9	0·05	0·05	
	A	0	120	180	15
Action	B	60	0	80	58
	C	90	40	0	83

The optimal act is still A and EOLI(I) = 15.

We proceed in exactly the same way for the possible forecasts of II and III, making the appropriate changes in probability.

COL table for forecast of outcome II

		Outcome			
		I	II	III	*EOL*
New probability		0·05	0·9	0·05	
	A	0	120	180	11·8 $\times \rightarrow$ 11·7
Action	B	60	0	80	7
	C	90	40	0	40·5

The optimal act remains unchanged at B and EOLI(II) = 7.
Similarly for a forecast of III.

COL table for forecast of outcome III

		Outcome			
		I	II	III	*EOL*
New probability		0·05	0·05	0·9	
	A	0	120	180	168
Action	B	60	0	80	75
	C	90	40	0	5·3 6·5

Once again the optimal act is not altered (this is not always the case, as we shall see) and EOLI(III) = 5·3.

We now know what the EOLI will be for any possible report from the consultant but we have not yet solved the problem of deciding whether to buy the report or not. It seems, that without buying the report we cannot decide whether to buy it though from the EOLI's it looks like a fairly promising prospect, even using the rule of thumb of not paying more than half the EVPI and applying it to the EVSI. How can we finally settle the issue?

The Heath Robinson Engineering Company cannot know *what* the consultant will forecast without buying his report but they can, as it were, *forecast* his forecast. They themselves have said that they feel the probabilities of models I, II, and III being chosen by the airlines are respectively 0·5, 0·2, and 0·3. Assuming that the consultant is some good and will work to the best of his ability the Heath Robinson Engineering Company must assume that these probabilities are *also* the probabilities of the three possible forecasts the consultant could make. If, for example, they felt that there was a 50% chance of the airlines adopting model I, 20% for model II, and 30% for model III, and at the same time thought there was an 80% chance that this skilful and reputable consultant would forecast model I, 10% that he would predict model II, and 10% for him saying model III then the Heath Robinson Engineering Company would be in a position which was, logically, complete nonsense. This would not be a new experience for them but a rational man would be forced to conclude that the two sets of probabilities had to be the same.

We can, therefore, complete the calculation by combining EOLI(I), EOLI(II), and EOLI(III) into an overall EOLI by weighting them by their probabilities. This is the same kind of process as calculating an expected value or an EOL. We get

$$EOLI = 0.5 \times 15 + 0.2 \times 7 + 0.3 \times 5.3$$
$$= 10.49$$

The original minimum EOL was 53 so we have

$$EVSI = \text{minimum EOL} - EOLI$$
$$= 53 - 10.49$$
$$= 42.51$$

which we take to be 42·5.

The consultant's fee was to be 20 m.u. which is just less than half of the EVSI so that, on the rule of thumb, the consultant's study should just about qualify for purchase.

There is, however, an alternative consultant who is not so good but a lot cheaper. His success rate is 60% and his fee is negotiable. How much should the Heath Robinson Engineering Company be prepared to pay for this forecast?

Again, we have to assume that the consultant's errors are equally divided. We get:

COL table for forecast of outcome I

		Outcome			
		I	II	III	*EOL*
New probability		0·6	0·2	0·2	
	A	0	120	180	60
Action	B	60	0	80	52
	C	90	40	0	62

The optimal act has now changed to B with EOLI(I) = 52.

This is a rather strange result. It is that when the cheaper consultant has forecast that the airlines will buy aircraft I, the Heath Robinson Engineering Company should build machine B which is what they should do if they knew that the airlines were going to buy aircraft II. This is rather like buying advice in order to ignore it, which seems rather odd. The reason is that this consultant has a poor record and makes many mistakes. If he is wrong the opportunity losses are so large that the Heath Robinson Engineering Company could suffer quite badly. This is, in short, a situation in which the assumption of repeatability would have to be scrutinized very closely indeed. This re-examination of the assumption could lead to the conclusion that, in this case the Heath Robinson Engineering Company should use the minimax OL criterion (which was covered in Chapter 1) and ignore probabilities altogether. If they do they will still select action B. (Prove it!)

For the moment we assume that the Heath Robinson Engineering Company are satisfied that, for their business, the assumption of repeatability is so well justified and the drawbacks of minimax OL are so great that they proceed with the analysis of the EVSI for the cheaper consultant.

COL table for forecast of Outcome II

		Outcome			
		I	II	III	*EOL*
New probability		0·2	0·6	0·2	
	A	0	120	180	108
Action	B	60	0	80	28
	C	90	40	0	42

The optimal act stays at B with EOLI(II) = 28.

COL table for forecast of outcome III

		Outcome			
		I	II	III	*EOL*
New probability		0·2	0·2	0·6	
	A	0	120	180	132
Action	B	60	0	80	60
	C	90	40	0	26

Now EOLI(III) = 26 and the optimal act is C.
We now calculate the overall EOLI as

$$EOLI = 0·5 \times 52 + 0·2 \times 28 + 0·3 \times 26 = 39·4$$

and

$$EVSI = 53·0 - 39·4 = 13·6$$

Using the half-EVSI rule the maximum fee would be $0·5 \times 13·6 = 6·8$.

In practice, looking at the size of the errors he could make, the Heath Robinson Engineering Company might well be dubious about employing him at all.

The point of this exercise is to show that there is no such thing as the 'right' information to collect or buy. The phrase 'we must have the best advice money can buy' may be downright misleading. Even poor information has a value, and a price, and the purchase of any information, even if it is perfect, has to be seen in context as part of the overall decision. This can be seen by considering the case of a third consultant who has the distinction that whatever he forecasts is certain to be wrong. The calculations yield the following information.

COL table for forecast of outcome I

		Outcome			
		I	II	III	*EOL*
New probability		0	0·5	0·5	
	A	0	120	180	150
Action	B	60	0	80	40
	C	90	40	0	20

The optimal act is C and EOLI(I) = 20.

COL table for forecast of outcome II

		Outcome			
		I	II	III	EOL
New probability		0·5	0	0·5	
	A	0	120	180	90
Action	B	60	0	80	70
	C	90	40	0	45

The optimal act is C and EOLI(II)=45.

COL table for forecast of outcome III

		Outcome			
		I	II	III	EOL
New probability		0·5	0·5	0	
	A	0	120	180	60
Action	B	60	0	80	30
	C	90	40	0	65

The optimal act is B and EOLI(III)=30.
Overall we have

$$\text{EOLI} = 0\cdot5 \times 20 + 0\cdot2 \times 45 + 0\cdot3 \times 30 = 18$$

and

$$\text{EVSI} = 53 - 18 = 35$$

This man should be more highly paid than the second consultant! This staggering result is because this man can be relied on to reduce the COL table to two columns.

The reader may now feel that the man who should be paid highest of all is the one who knows how to do all these calculations. They become easier with practice and the reader should now feel that the calculations are worth the effort for the information they generate.

Problems

1. What is the EVPI in Problem 6, Chapter 3?

2. A decision problem can be expressed as

Pay off table

		Outcome			
		I	II	III	IV
Probability		0·2	0·4	0·3	0·1
	A	20	40	10	15
Action	B	30	10	40	−40
	C	25	20	30	−60

What is the EVPI?

3. In Problem 2 it is possible to get a prediction of the outcome which is 85% accurate. It costs 3 units to make the prediction. Is it worth it?

4. For the pay off table:

		Outcome			
		I	II	III	IV
	A	20	60	70	190
Action	B	40	30	90	20
	C	110	160	40	150
	D	80	70	30	120

What is the EVPI if the probabilities are 0·10, 0·20, 0·50, and 0·20 for outcomes I to IV respectively? What is it if the probabilities are taken in reverse order?

What are the managerial implications of the answer?

5. There is a market research method which can be used to forecast outcomes. It seems to be about 80% accurate and we wish to determine the EVSI in Problem 1 with a view to using it.

The method of apportioning the error equally among the other outcomes which was used in the chapter appears to be a bit sweeping when the error amounts to 20%. An alternative is to allocate the 20% in proportion to the original probability estimates for the remaining outcomes. For instance, if the forecast is for outcome I the original probability estimates for outcomes II, III, and IV were 0·50, 0·20, and 0·10. The 20% error in the forecast is then split by these proportions and the overall distribution is taken as:

Outcome	Probability
I	0·80 (this is the one which was forecast and 80% is the accuracy of the forecasting method)
II	$\dfrac{0·50}{0·50 + 0·20 + 0·10} \times 0·20 = 0·125$
III	$\dfrac{0·20}{0·50 + 0·20 + 0·10} \times 0·20 = 0·050$
IV	$\dfrac{0·10}{0·50 + 0·20 + 0·10} \times 0·20 = 0·025$

Notice that $0·125 + 0·05 + 0·025 = 0·20$, which is the error to be distributed.

Using this method for error allocation what is the EVSI for the market research?

8
Decision-making with continuous variables

8.1 Continuous and discrete variables

In earlier chapters we have studied problems in which, for example, demand for a product could be low, medium, or high. Perhaps in the circumstances 'low' means 5000 tons/month, 'medium' is 10000 tons/month, and 'high' is taken to be 20000 tons/month. Now, it is pretty clear that demand is not restricted to only these values and could very easily turn out to be, perhaps 18500 tons/month. In fact demand is, in reality, what is called a **continuous variable**, that is, it can take on any value at all over some range. For instance, there might be a minimum level of 3000 tons, below which demand simply could not sink because that is the consumption of those customers to whom the product is absolutely essential. Similarly, it might be impossible for demand to be more than 25000 tons because at that level everybody who could remotely use the product would be buying it. In between 3000 and 25000 demand could, in principle, vary in minutely small steps if we are prepared to allow for fractions of a ton and could, therefore, be 3000, 3000·0001, and so on, up to 25000.

The opposite to a continuous variable is a **discrete** variable which is only allowed to have a certain number of fixed values. For instance, the number of children in a family can only be 0, 1, 2, etc. It is unusual to find more than about five children in a family and most discrete variables are in fact limited to a fairly small number of fixed values.

The dividing line between continuous and discrete variables is fairly indistinct in practice, though not in theory. For example, if we were only prepared to deal in 10-ton units in the earlier example, the variable of demand would become discrete because it would be limited to the values 3000, 3010, 3020, and so on. In practice, we might still regard it as continuous for many purposes because there are very many possible values and they are fairly close to one another. The effect of this kind of approximation is often that we can choose to regard a variable as continuous or discrete according to whichever is the more convenient form.

So far in the book we have implicitly assumed that the problem structure was such that the discrete form was appropriate and a reasonable approximation to reality. This is often perfectly valid and, as long as the results are interpreted with reasonable care, no difficulty need arise. Inevitably, however, cases will occur where it simply is not sufficiently accurate to lump a continuous variable into three or four categories and regard it as discrete and we then have to take account of the fact that it really is continuous. This chapter deals with two principal ways out of the impasse—continuous analysis and detailed approximation.

8.2 The essentials of continuous analysis

The essential feature of the continuous form of analysis is that the probabilities have to be put into an appropriate form called a **continuous distribution**. From this point, the calculation proceeds using mathematical methods or fairly refined arithmetic to determine answers of the type that we have found in earlier chapters for the discrete case.

The main features of a continuous distribution will first be examined and then we shall discuss some of the managerial implications of continuous analysis.

8.3 Continuous distributions

We approach a continuous distribution by first considering a discrete distribution. Suppose that a variable can vary continuously between 5000 and 20000. This range can be divided up into three sub-ranges 5000–10000,

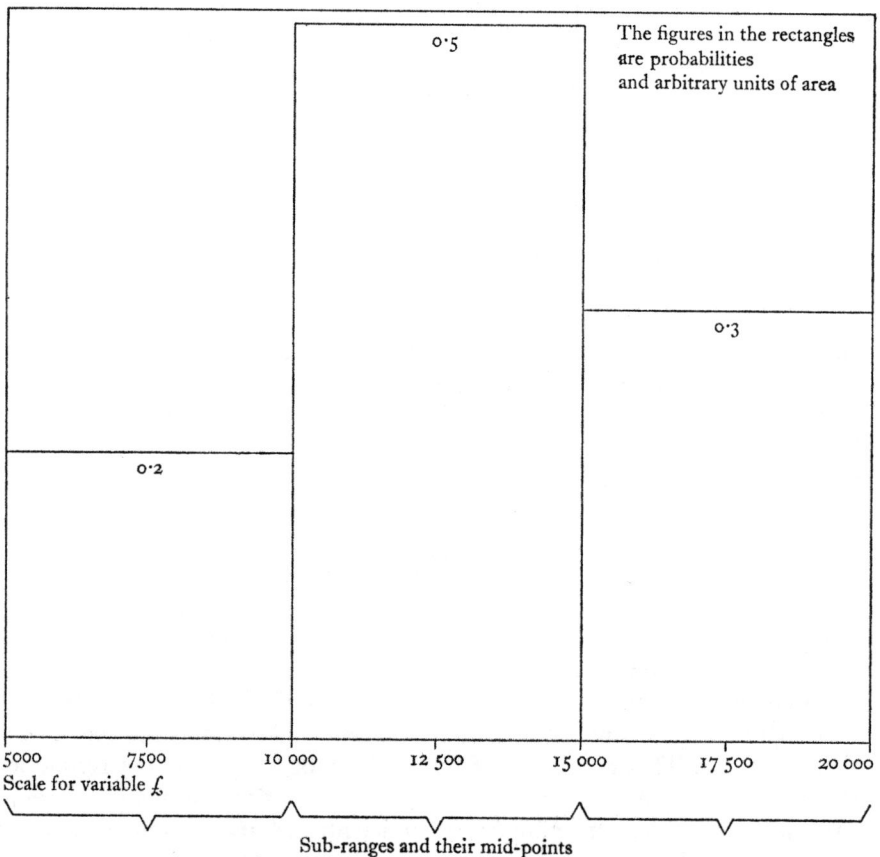

Fig. 8.1 A probability histogram

10000–15000, and 15000–20000. The mid-points of these sub-ranges are 7500, 12500, and 17500, so we could get a very rough approximation to the actual continuous variable by treating it as a discrete variable limited to these three values. Suppose, the probabilities of the three discrete values were 0·2, 0·5, and 0·3 then we could represent the distribution diagrammatically as in Fig. 8.1.

This kind of diagram is called a **histogram** and it is widely used in statistical work. Unlike ordinary graphs in which the height of the graph line is the important feature, a histogram is based on **areas**. The three rectangles in Fig. 8.1 have areas which are 0·2, 0·5, and 0·3 square units respectively. In this particular histogram, all the rectangles have the same length in their bases and therefore, their heights are also proportional to the probabilities represented by the rectangles. This need not be the case and the rectangles' bases may vary so that, in general, the height of the rectangle has no significance and may be downright misleading. For this reason, a histogram is never drawn with a vertical scale in the way that a graph always is. The histogram has to be interpreted visually by trying to compare areas, and this is not always easy.

The main advantage of the histogram in probability work is that, as the areas of the rectangles are proportional to probabilities, the total area of the three rectangles is proportional to 1·00 units of area which is the total probability. The rectangles also denote that the probability of the variable being, say, between 5000 and 10000 is to be regarded as the same as the probability of it having the approximate mid-range value of 7500, namely, 0·2.

Now, this approximation is probably pretty inadequate and we could make

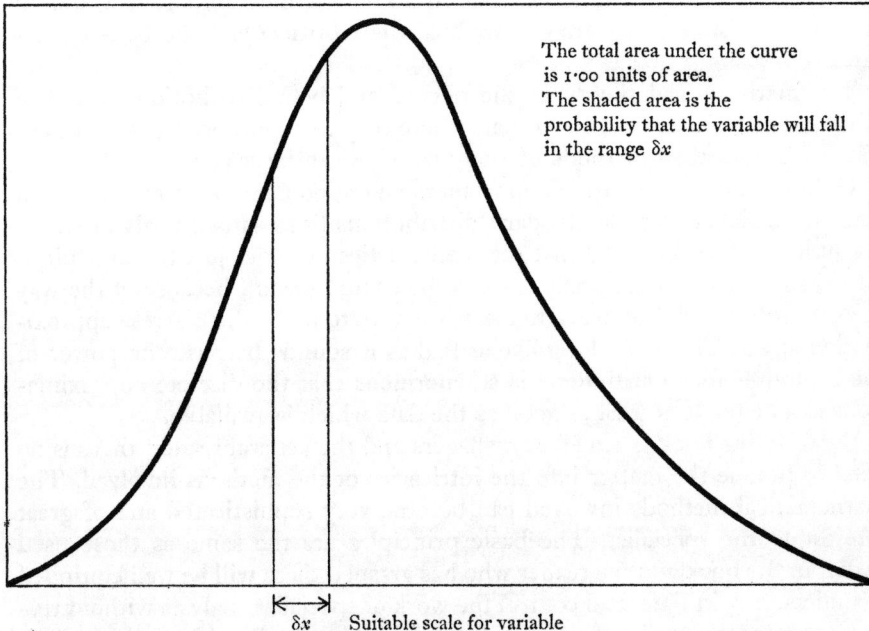

The total area under the curve is 1·00 units of area.
The shaded area is the probability that the variable will fall in the range δx

δx Suitable scale for variable

Fig. 8.2 A probability curve

it better by having perhaps 10 sub-ranges and apportioning the probability to the 10 mid-range values. The diagram would be the same as Fig. 8.1 except that there would be 10 rectangles but the total area of these rectangles would still have to be 1·00 units of area. The probability of the variable falling in any particular sub-range would still be taken to be the probability of the mid-point and the analysis would continue to be in the discrete form.

The approximation could be steadily improved by using more and more sub-ranges until eventually the tops of the rectangles blended into a smooth curve such as Fig. 8.2. The effect of the process is that the area under the curve would still be 1·00 which corresponds to the proper total probability. Methods exist which enable one to calculate areas under all, or part, of such a curve so no problem arises there.

With such a continuous distribution curve it becomes impossible to speak of the probability of the variable having any particular value because when we take a particular value this is tantamount to making the rectangle so thin that it becomes a line and a line has no area. We can, however, determine the probability that the variable will fall in an interval such as δx (read 'delta x' and meaning a small step in the variable's range) this being the proportion of the total area under the curve which lies in the strip just above δx. We can calculate this area by one of several methods.

8.4 Using continuous distributions

There are, of course, very many possible shapes which a curve such as Fig. 8.2 could have. In practice, it turns out that there are a few standard shapes which occur very frequently in practice or which are very good approximations to real-life probability distributions. The two most important standard curves in decision theory are the **normal distribution** and the **beta distribution**.

The mathematical theory of the normal and beta distributions has been fairly extensively developed so that, where they are appropriate, one can use direct mathematical methods of analysis. This can be very useful.

Unfortunately, there are circumstances where no amount of mathematical skill will make one of the standard distributions fit as satisfactorily or where the problem is so involved that the mathematics becomes just too difficult to do. In such cases we naturally turn to the computer but, because of the way the computer works, in order to use it we have to make the discrete approximation again. This is nothing like as bad as it sounds because the power of the computer to do arithmetic is so enormous that the discrete approximations can be made at least as good as the data which is available.

Because this book is aimed at managers and the general reader, there is no need to pursue the matter into the intricacies of the methods involved. The mathematical methods involved can become very sophisticated and of great interest to the specialist. The basic principles are the same as those used earlier in the book and the reader who has grasped these will be well equipped to understand, initiate, and control the work of specialist analysts without trying to master the details of their professional skills as well as his own.

Before leaving the subject, however, we would do well to examine the way in which an assessment of probabilities for the discrete approximation can be transformed into something approaching a continuous form of distribution— a process known as **smoothing**.

8.5 Smoothing probabilities

The Heath Robinson Engineering Company, having narrowly survived its involvement in the aircraft industry, is now trying to develop a machine for packaging newspapers. The economics of the project depend very heavily on just how expensive it will prove to be to make the machine reach its design speed. The refinement of a complicated machine is a protracted process and may involve testing, redesign, machining of new parts, and re-assembly. Depending on just how many problems have to be ironed out, the process may have to be repeated many times and the cost could be anywhere from £10000 to £60000. Having had some experience of engineering development work, the Chief Engineer thinks that the best guess he can make is that the cost might be in the range £10000–£20000 with a probability of 0·2 and a 50% probability of the cost being in the range £20000–£30000. Failing either of these it has to be in the range £30000–£60000, i.e., the probability would

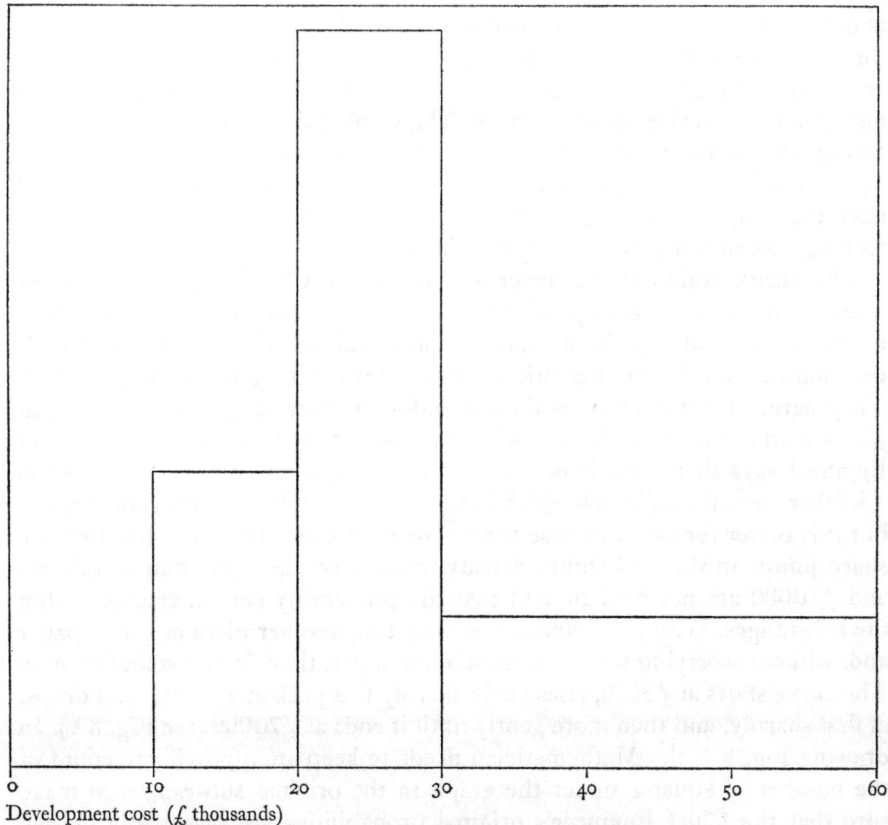

Fig. 8.3 The Heath Robinson Engineering Company's first histogram

FDA

be 0·3. He is absolutely unwilling to give a more detailed estimate than that but the information he will give is simply on too coarse a scale to be of any use at all in decision analysis. How should the Heath Robinson Engineering Company proceed?

Having no idea of what to do they hire a mathematician, who can always be blamed if things go wrong. He in turn will blame either the data he was given or the way the probabilities turned out but first he calculates in a number of stages. The first task is to draw Fig. 8.3 which represents the 'data' of the probabilities as a histogram like Fig. 8.1. In drawing the histogram we notice that the three sub-ranges are not all equal, and there is no reason why they have to be. They can be chosen to fit the problem in hand. The first two sub-ranges have an equal 'span' of £10000 while the third has a span of £30000 or three times as much. In drawing the histogram we can take advantage of this in order to save a lot of tedious calculations in working out areas (recall the nature of a histogram). In the first two sub-ranges we have to draw rectangles which are respectively proportional in area to 0·2 and 0·5 but as they have equal bases we can get this result just as easily by making the heights of the rectangles proportional to 0·2 and 0·5, respectively. The actual unit of area does not matter and can be quite arbitrary—what matters is the proportions of the areas, not their actual size. The third rectangle has to have an area of 0·3 units but its base is three times the length of those of the first two rectangles. Again, we can get the required area proportion by making the height of the block proportional to 0·3 ÷ 3 or 0·1 measured in any convenient units of height. This is simply a dodge and does not alter the idea of a histogram as a device based on areas. The whole thing can now be drawn by taking one square of graph paper horizontally to represent £10000 and one square vertically to be proportional to 0·1 height units. The end result will have the proper area proportions and in each sub-range the height of the rectangle implies the 'probability density'.

The Heath Robinson Engineering Company's Chief Engineer and their Mathematician look at Fig. 8.3 and agree that it does not reflect the true position. Actually, it is a faithful portrayal of the Chief Engineer's probabilities but the Mathematician does not think it tactful to dwell on that. They agree that the chances do not suddenly start at £10000 and end at £60000 and there is really a gradual build-up and dying-away. The Chief Engineer says that there is no chance of development costs being less than £5000 or more than £70000 which is a little different from his previous figures, but it is better for him to revise them now than later. They also feel that the sharp jumps in the probability density implied by the histogram at £20000 and £30000 are not realistic and that the probability should change within the sub-ranges. With this information they take another piece of graph paper and, without worrying for the present about areas, they draw a smooth curve. The curve starts at £5000, rises fairly sharply to a peak at £25000, and drops, at first sharply, and then more gently until it ends at £70000 (see Fig. 8.4). In drawing Fig. 8.4, the Mathematician needs to keep an approximate count of the number of squares under the graph in the original sub-ranges to make sure that the Chief Engineer's original probabilities are reasonably closely followed.

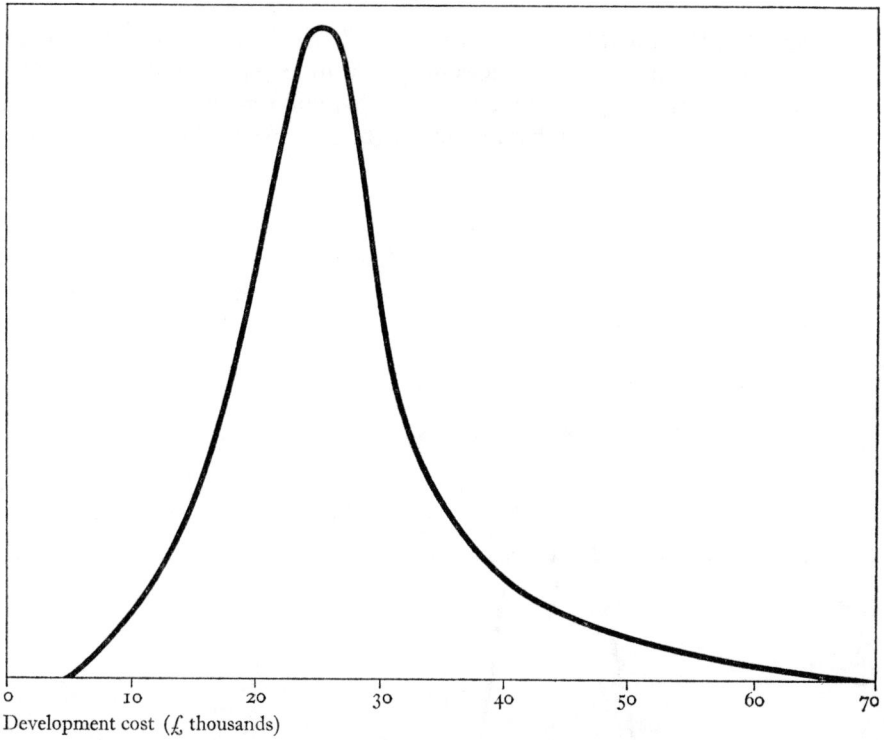

Fig. 8.4 The Heath Robinson Engineering Company's smooth curve

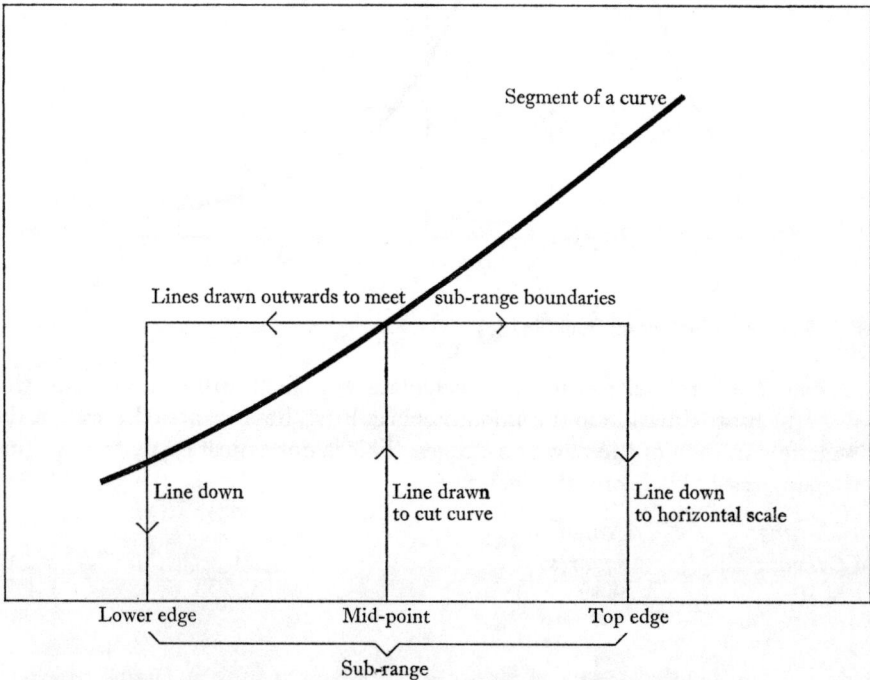

Fig. 8.5 Detail of the construction of a histogram from a smooth curve

Having got the smooth curve of Fig. 8.4 it is decided to adopt the discrete approximation, but with sub-ranges of £5000 to give accuracy. The Mathematician now draws Fig. 8.6 by taking Fig. 8.4 and drawing a vertical line at the centre of each £5000 sub-range until the line meets the curve. He then draws a horizontal line from this meeting point going left and right until the horizontal line meets the vertical graph-paper markings at the ends of the particular sub-range. From these points he draws lines down to the development-cost axis to complete a rectangle. This procedure is shown in detail on an expanded scale in Fig. 8.5 and the final result, without the detailed lines of the geometrical construction, in Fig. 8.6.

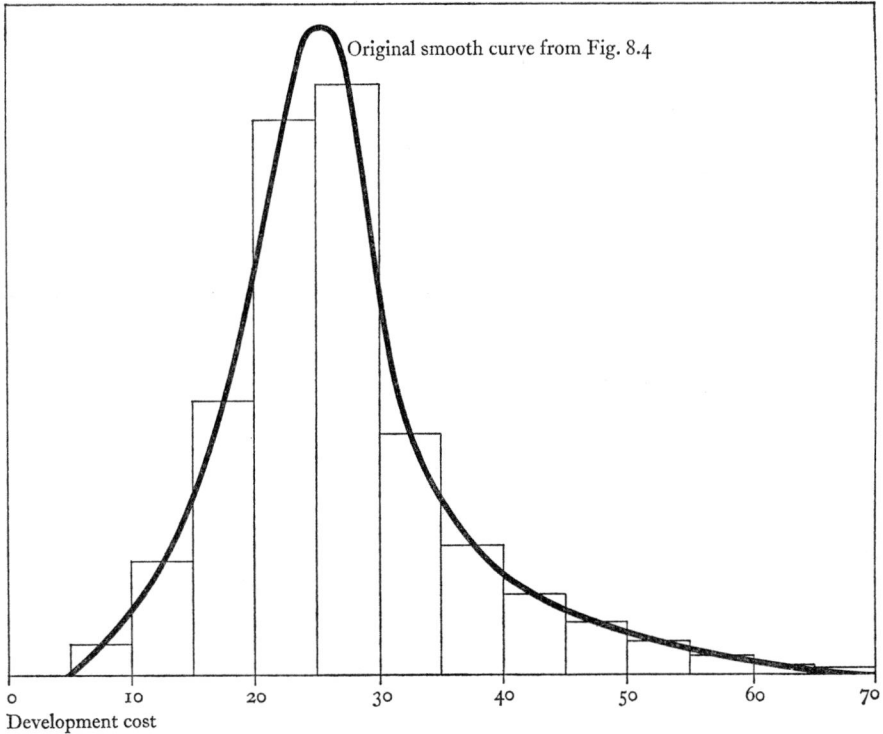

Original smooth curve from Fig. 8.4

Development cost

Fig. 8.6 Final histogram from Fig. 8.4

The Mathematician can now calculate the final probabilities for this discrete approximation to the smooth curve. First, he measures the area of the rectangle in each of the new sub-ranges. This is done most easily by counting the squares in each one. He gets:

Sub-range (£ thousand)	No. of squares
5–10	0·4
10–15	1·5
15–20	4·4
20–25	8·7
25–30	9·3

Sub-Range	No. of
(£ thousand)	squares
30–35	3·8
35–40	2·2
40–45	1·2
45–50	0·8
50–55	0·6
55–60	0·4
60–65	0·2
65–70	0·1

Total 33·6

Now, if 33·6 squares are to represent a probability of 1·00 then the probability to be assigned to the sub-range 30–35, which has 3·8 squares, must be

$$\frac{3·8}{33·6} = 0·113$$

Applying this process to the list of area yields a table of probabilities:

Sub-range	Probability
5–10	0·012
10–15	0·045
15–20	0·131
20–25	0·259
25–30	0·276
30–35	0·113
35–40	0·065
40–45	0·036
45–50	0·024
50–55	0·018
55–60	0·012
60–65	0·006
65–70	0·003

1·000

It should be borne in mind that these probabilities are given to three decimal places simply because many of them are so small that otherwise they would be ignored. We have not trebled the accuracy of the data by doing this rather arbitrary calculation.

A simple check may now be done to see how well the revised figures correspond to the Chief Engineer's original probability distribution. By adding together the values of the appropriate sub-ranges the Mathematician finds the values 0·188, 0·535, and 0·277 compared with 0·2, 0·5, and 0·3. This correspondence is fairly close especially when it is remembered that the original values have no special claim to precision. If the agreement between the original and final probabilities is not good enough, either overall or in detail, the final probabilities can easily be changed by making the offending part of Fig. 8.4 higher or lower, to increase or decrease the value respectively, and then recalculating. The amount of recalculation is trivial with a little practice. It would, in fact, be possible to automate the whole process and program a computer to take an initial probability assessment and produce revised distributions from it until one was found which was deemed to be satisfactory.

The reader is quite right if he is thinking that this whole process lacks some of the purity which he has been taught in the past to associate with mathematical analysis. The fact of the matter is that mathematics is a system of reasoning which, when applied to precise problems will lead to 'right' answers. In managerial decision-making the problem is rarely completely precise. Much depends on judgement and experience. The aim of decision theory is to try to supply some aids to the process of decision-making especially where the decision situation involves uncertainty. The idea is that, by providing the analytical framework, the manager will be able to concentrate on supplying the human inputs of intuition and experience one by one without having to try to juggle these in his head, whilst at the same time trying to provide further inputs.

8.6 Loss functions

We have examined how simple probability statements can be converted into smoothed distributions but how are we to make use of them?

The simplest way of using a smoothed distribution is merely to work out the pay off or opportunity loss associated with the mid-point of each sub-range in the smoothed distribution and then to calculate an expected value in the usual way.

For instance, the Heath Robinson Engineering Company have estimated that, before allowing for development costs the present value of their profit from the newspaper packaging machine will be £31 000. They are sure of this because they have contracts to sell a particular number of machines at a fixed price and their only uncertainty is how much it will cost to make the machine work.

The easiest way of calculating the outcome is to work out the expected value of the development cost and compare it with the revenue figure. The EV of the development cost is the total of the mid-points of the sub-ranges multiplied by the corresponding probabilities, i.e., $7500 \times 0 \cdot 012 + 12500 \times 0 \cdot 045 + 17500 \times 0 \cdot 131$, and so on. This comes out to £27 355 approximately so there is an expected pay off of £31 000 − £27 355 = £3645. This might or might not be large enough to induce the Heath Robinson Engineering Company to undertake the work.

Another way of solving the same problem is by means of a **loss function**. This is an equation or table showing how losses and profits depend on the outcome. For example, if the outcome is, that the development cost is £12 500 then the profit to the Heath Robinson Engineering Company will be £31 000 − £12 500 = £18 500. Similarly, if the outcome is a development cost of £57 500 the profit will be £31 000 − £57 500 = − £26 500, i.e., a loss. Notice, that we always assume the outcome is at the mid-point of the sub-range. This is a consequence of the discrete approximation but providing the sub-ranges are not too wide the error is not very serious.

We can now calculate the loss table as follows.

Sub-range £ thousands	Mid-point £	Outcome £
5–10	7500	23 500
10–15	12 500	18 500
15–20	17 500	13 500
20–25	22 500	8500
25–30	27 500	3500
30–35	32 500	– 1500
35–40	37 500	– 6500
40–45	42 500	– 11 500
45–50	47 500	– 16 500
50–55	52 500	– 21 500
55–60	57 500	– 26 500
60–65	62 500	– 31 500
65–70	67 500	– 36 50C

We now calculate the expected value of the outcome by multiplying each entry in the third column of this table by the corresponding probability and adding. We have $23\,500 \times 0{\cdot}012 + 18\,500 \times 0{\cdot}045 + 13\,500 \times 0{\cdot}131$, and so forth, and the result is £3645 as before. It can be proved, and it is intuitively obvious, that these two calculations lead to the same result.

Calculated in this way the loss-function concept has no great appeal because it inevitably involved a little more work. It becomes more useful when used with opportunity losses which are already in the form of a loss function.

The idea of a loss function can be shown quite effectively in a diagram such as Fig. 8.7 which is drawn for a truly continuous distribution. The horizontal scale is drawn to suit the stochastic variable—in the last example this was development cost but it can be anything, such as demand, labour performance, machine speed, etc. On this scale the point O is the break-even point – £31 000 in the last example, the vertical scale is for profit *and* loss and the lines OA′ and OB′ show how profit and loss grow as the stochastic variable departs from the break-even point.

If the diagram were to show the break-even point of profit and fixed cost then OB′ would be a profit line, B would be the profit side of the diagram, OA′ would be a loss line, and A would be the loss side of the diagram.

In the last example we had development cost versus profit so OB′ would be a loss line and OA′ a profit line (and the peak of the distribution curve would lie to the left of the break-even line). The point is that the chart is drawn to suit the problem, and the lines OA′ and OB′ need not slope up equally steeply— they also depend on the problem.

It might be argued that whichever of OA′ and OB′ is, the loss line should be shown below the horizontal axis to show that it is a loss. This is not done because the probability distribution is an essential feature of the diagram and that has to be drawn above the line. Once one gets used to this convention it becomes very clear that Fig. 8.7 is indeed a break-even chart but because it

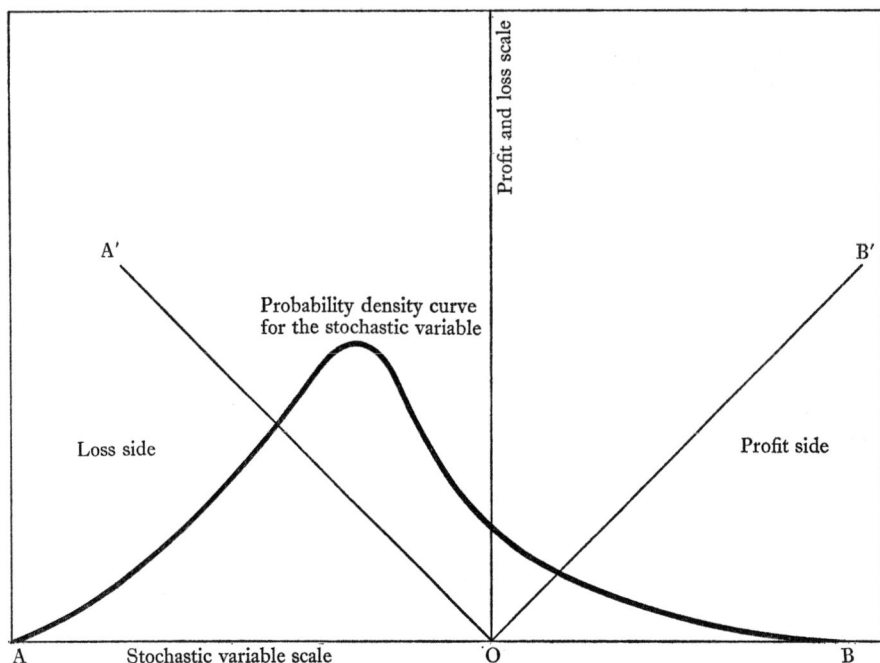

Note: 1. The profit sides may be interchanged depending on the definition of the stochastic variable.

2. The peak of the probability density curve may not lie over point O at which the stochastic variable changes from profit- to loss-making values.

Fig. 8.7 The loss function idea

shows probabilities it is a big improvement on the conventional form of a break-even chart. In the case of Fig. 8.7, if OB′ is a profit line and although losses can mount very steeply, it is fairly clear that we should have an *expected* profit because the bulk of the probability distribution lies on the profit side of break even.

If we are in a position to use a standard continuous distribution such as the normal distribution it is possible to make use of standard tables, called N(D) tables, which give the expected profit or loss directly, without calculation. Without explaining the theory of the normal distribution we cannot explain the calculations though they are far from difficult. The loss functions in Fig. 8.7 were linear, that is, their graphs were straight lines. There is no need to limit ourselves in this way, and by analogy with the arguments advanced for the use of utility, we might wish to bend the loss function so that there was a large penalty for being very far from break even. This applies particularly on the loss side and the effect is to make projects involving the risk of loss show up rather badly in the analysis, thereby making them less likely to be selected. Precisely the same result could be achieved by using utility in the first place, rather than cash. The main difficulty about this seems to be the psychological one of persuading people to think in terms of utility.

Problems

1. The Heath Robinson Engineering Company have decided to join forces with the Hopeless Transport Company in building and operating a ready-mixed concrete plant. They assess the volume of demand as:

Loads per year	Probability
0–10 000	0·3
10 000–20 000	0·4
20 000–30 000	0·3

The plant has a capacity of 30 000 loads/year so there is no point in going any higher than that.

The Heath Robinson Engineering Company are now quite sophisticated in decision theory and they hire you to smooth the distribution into classes with ranges of 2500 loads. When you remark that this is a bit of a vague instruction they add that there is certain to be some demand, even for a product made by the Heath Robinson Engineering Company, and there is even a chance that there will be more demand than the plant can handle.

2. The fixed cost of the Heath Robinson Engineering Company Plant will be £150 000 per year and the marginal profit will be £10/load. Using the loss-function idea what is the expected value of the project?

3. One of the few sure things about projects of any kind is that they hardly ever achieve their plans exactly.

Heath Robinson are trying to promote another new product and they are worried about whether demand will exceed the break even point. The marketing manager has assessed probabilities that demand will prove to be within certain percentages of the break-even point as follows:

Range	Probability
−30% to −10%	0·40
−10% to +10%	0·10
+10% to +30%	0·50

After a lot of argument the marketing director agrees that the worst that could happen is that demand could be as low as 40% below break-even and the best is that it could be 50% above. He adds that he feels the probabilities fall off very sharply outside the ranges given in the table and there is practically no chance that demand will be exactly at the break-even level.

Smooth the demand into segments with a width of 10% (i.e., from 0 to 10% and so on).

4. The loss function in Problem 3 is such that losses increase more and more rapidly as demand falls below break-even, while profits rise proportionately as demand rises above break-even. The loss in profit is measured in monetary units per 1% difference between demand and break-even, as shown in the following table

Demand differs from break-even by an amount in the range	Rate of pay off in money units per 1% difference between demand and break-even
−40% to −30%	−2
−30% to −20%	−1·5
−20% to 0%	−1
0% to 50%	+1·25

This means that if demand later turns out to be −24% the pay off will be −24 × 1·5 = −36. While if it is −37% the pay off will be −37 × 2 = −74 and so on. What is the expected value of the project?

9

Decision theory in practice

9.1 Introduction

In the previous eight chapters we have covered the principal features of decision theory showing how the theory worked, explaining the manner of doing the calculations, and discussing the interpretation of the answers. We have not explored the deeper mathematical reaches of the theory mainly because we wished to argue that decision theory is something the manager can use in daily practice. Indeed, most managers could not be expected to have the time to master the more advanced (and frankly very difficult) mathematics involved. This implies that the simple and easily learned techniques are of far more practical use than the advanced mathematical analysis and this is indeed the case in all but the most complex situations. In such circumstances the manager can always call on the services of a specialist in the field and, if the manager understands and can use the simple methods, he is much more likely to get some actual benefit from the work of the specialist than if he proceeds in virtual ignorance of decision theory.

We stated quite openly at the beginning of the book that the reader would have to make up his own mind, by working through the material, just what practical use the techniques of decision theory could be, in his particular situation. The variety of circumstances in business is so wide that it is certainly true that there are situations where the use of decision theory could be not only a waste of effort but downright misleading. The typical example would be in industrial relations where negotiations are proceeding in such a way that there is a distinct possibility of a damaging strike or a crippling increase in labour costs caused by too high a wage settlement. One could only agree with the manager who contended that in such an impasse he was better employed in more effective negotiation than in calculating pay offs from probabilities of various lengths of strike or sizes of wage settlement. This is one extreme. At the other end of the scale there are decisions to do with the purchase of machinery, production planning, and quality control which, though not less important to the firm than the industrial relations example, are more clear-cut, have better data (or at least more of it which is often thought to be the same thing), and naturally lend themselves to the kind of probabilistic analysis we have been presenting.

Unfortunately, the great bulk of managerial decisions lies between these two extremes. The types of decision involved cover the whole span of managerial activity—production, marketing, finance, and corporate planning, for example—and the complete range from data-rich clarity to virtual obscurity of the issues, choices, and facts. Is decision theory of any practical value for such problems? The purpose of this chapter is to try to help the reader to make up his own mind about the merits of each particular case by focusing on some of the questions which must have come into his mind as he has read about the arithmetical techniques. First, we shall have to say what we mean by 'practical value' and then we shall examine some of the conceptual and practical problems in more detail.

Before dwelling on the practicalities we must, however, make quite clear that the whole thread of the argument in this book is that decision theory is something which most managers will find to be of practical use on most of the days they are at work. The reader who has come to agree with that proposition will be in the uncomfortable position of having to follow up his agreement with enough hard work to master at least the rudimentary techniques described in this book. He may take some comfort from the fact that, despite what he may now feel, the arithmetic is not all that difficult or laborious. We shall deal with this in more detail under the heading of 'The use of specialists'. First we return to the position outlined at the end of the last paragraph.

9.2 Practical value

We have suggested that decision theory is a set of tools to which the manager should devote some effort because they would be of 'practical value' in his daily work. The trouble about this statement is that the meaning of 'practical value' varies from case to case and, more importantly, from individual to individual. What, then, have we taken it to mean in this book?

Although decision theory is not really part of the group of methods called 'operational research' it is worth looking at the utility of the latter in order to throw some light on the 'practical-value' question. There are many definitions of operational research—most of them involving concepts such as 'the use of scientific or mathematical analysis in business problems'. By far the best definition is, however, 'the art of giving bad answers to questions to which otherwise worse answers would be given'. This will serve very well as a simple, and only slightly facetious, definition of decision theory. By this definition, decision theory is a means of improving on managerial decisions and in this sense it is of practical value. The improvement comes from five main directions—very roughly in order of importance:

Treatment of uncertainty

Clarity of assumptions

Comprehensiveness

Consistency

Specialist techniques

Treatment of uncertainty

Anyone with the slightest practical knowledge of business must agree that the future is an uncertain place to be. Several examples have already been given but one more may help, at the risk of labouring the point. The publishers of this book have great experience in the field and a creditable record. At the same time, they commit themselves to the very heavy expense of publication without knowing what the eventual sales will be. Certainly, they cannot sell more than they produce and it would seem safe not to produce too many. However, the fixed costs are very high and the variable cost comparatively low so they do not wish to forego additional profits. At the same time it is not unknown for publishers to be left with unsold stocks on their hands. The uncertainty can be reduced by printing only a few books to start with and then reprinting if the demand warrants it. This, however, leaves them open to the risk of not having books in stock at the time of greatest demand, namely, the start of the academic year. The problem is rather more involved than this but the fact remains that it is strewn with major and minor areas of uncertainty. The use of decision theory offers a formal and systematic way of incorporating the uncertainties into the decision problem.

The reader may well ask why we should worry about formality and system when it is abundantly clear that decision theory, of itself, does nothing to remove or reduce uncertainty and the manager who uses it has to rely at least as heavily as he ever did on the undefinable but real qualities of flair and judgement. The advantage of formality is that it calls for judgement to be exercised in a context which is well defined, clearly stated, and, if this book and others like it have served their purpose, well understood. For example, using the theory of expected value, the manager's intuition is focussed not on a wide-ranging question of 'what should we do' but on the probabilities to be attached to various outcomes. Using a decision tree enables the manager to concentrate, not on 'what should we do now?', but on 'what are the other things we could do if such-and-such happens'. At each stage the assumptions he should make and the questions to be answered are clearly worked out. The problem can be approached in a formal manner and the whole process can be checked and reviewed more easily to ensure that nothing has been left out and that reasonable assumptions have been made.

This point leads us very naturally and imperceptibly into the advantages of the systematic approach. The idea of a systematic approach is very similar to the economists' notion of the division of labour but in this case the division may be between several people or among the various facets of the work which one man is called on to do. The result of using decision theory is that the manager concentrates his thoughts on one part of the decision at a time rather than trying to balance in his mind all the many aspects of the problem at the same time. Thus, he has to think in turn of what the outcomes might be, what the probabilities are (when he is using expected values), and finally, a few arithmetical steps bring him to a formalized and systematic conclusion. The whole process may take anything from a couple of minutes to as many years depending on the nature of the problem and the amount of data involved. The whole process of analysis and conclusion may be accomplished on the back of an envelope or with the aid of a 200-page report and a couple of hours on a large computer but that is a result of the complexity of the problem and the level of management involved. It has nothing to do with the applicability of decision theory which prescribes much the same steps for all decisions—another advantage of the formality and the systematic approach in the treatment of uncertainty.

Clarity of assumptions

Suppose, two managers, A and B, respectively support and oppose a project which will generate a profit of 100 if it succeeds and a loss of 100 (i.e., a profit of − 100) if it fails. Now, either they have different information about the project and the factors which will determine its success or failure or, they have the same information and have drawn different conclusions from it. Either way, it is fairly obvious in this case that A feels the project is more likely to succeed than fail and that B holds the opposite view.

We reached the foregoing conclusion by knowing A's and B's respective attitudes and with the aid of some information about the outcome pay offs and an elementary knowledge of the concept of expected value. We did not know whether A or B had used expected value ideas, what their probabilities were, or whether A had even considered the probability of failure or B that of success. In view of this, a third person, C, called on to take sides in the dispute would have rather a hard task to make up his mind about whether A or B had made the correct assumptions. (We ignore for simplicity the possibility that A is C's boss and doesn't like to be crossed and similar behavioural snags.) If C would find it hard in this very simple case what are the difficulties likely to be in the far more complex world of real life?

Apart from considerations of the firms politics the main trouble is that nobody's assumptions (A's, B's, *or* C's) have been made clear. The second great advantage of the use of decision theory is that assumptions about outcomes and particularly about the probabilities to be associated with them have to be made abundantly clear, at clearly defined stages in the analysis. Thus, in the previous example, if A declares that the probability of success is 90% and B feels that it is 20% then the area of their disagreement is plain for a third person to see. If the importance of the decision warrants it then a further series of questions can be asked. Has one man got more or different information? Does his experience qualify him better to judge? Have they simply put down some numbers which they do not understand or believe, simply in order to persuade the decision theorist to go away and let them get on with something more important? If the latter is true was it the right thing to do in the circumstances? (It sometimes is!)

Notice, that there is no virtue in getting A and B to compromise at 55% (which is the average of 90% and 20%) just for the sake of agreement. For one thing A would still get his way because, if expected value is the proper criterion, the project will still go ahead. Furthermore, if they do agree on 55% and the project is initiated then whatever the outcome either A or B can ascribe it to the way the probabilities turned out and not to failures in his own judgement. Notice also, that if they agreed in recommending the initiation of the project because A thought that the probability of success was 90% and B felt that 60% was more appropriate then there might well not be much point in attempting to close the gap or in trying to find the reasons for their disagreement.

Whatever the situation the use of decision theory does force assumptions into the open. If divergences are found then there are several remedies depending on the circumstances. The disagreement about probabilities may be as a result of differences in training, experience, available information, or temperamental suitability for a decision-making role.

If A, as at the beginning of the example, supports the project while B rejects it this may be due to the reasons examined above or it may be that A is saying, in effect, 'the project is certain to be a success because I can make it work' while B is saying the opposite. If this is the case, then the personal problems are best left to the imagination of the experienced reader. The act of writing down a 100% or 0% probability may well provide a clue to what is being assumed.

It may also indicate a poor analysis of the problem. As we have pointed out, many projects can be made successful providing enough is put into them. The uncertainty then falls on the costs of the project. To assume that a profit of 100 is certain to be achieved implies that costs can be held to a definite level in the face of uncertainty. Now, this implies either that the project is exceedingly simple, the manager is phenomenally talented, or that he has a very naïve approach to business uncertainty.

A little earlier in this discussion we said that A or B could always blame an outcome which cast doubt on his judgement regarding the way in which the probabilities had turned out. Thus, B says there is only a 20% chance of success but if the project is initiated against his judgement and does succeed he can always say that he didn't say that it *wouldn't* succeed merely that it was unlikely to. Clearly, the idea of repeatability will not allow him to use this justification too often but the escape clause always exists and its presence is a psychological disadvantage to the use of decision theory. We return to this problem in the discussion of repeatability later in this chapter. For the moment we note that human nature is such that, if the project is pushed ahead and fails, B will probably say 'I told you so'. Naturally, A would say the same thing about the success of the project while blaming the probabilities if it failed. If the person responsible for supervising A and B has heard of repeatability he will watch outcomes and compare them with the probabilities A and B stated in their decision analyses and use the results to monitor the job performance of A and B. The ability to generate that kind of information, imperfect though it would be, is a useful side benefit of decision theory.

Comprehensiveness

The use of decision theory, apart from the major advantages of treatment of uncertainty and clarity of assumptions, has the additional advantage of ensuring almost automatically that all the outcomes have been considered. This does not arise from the particular techniques themselves but from the questions they raise in the mind of the user when they are intelligently employed. There was an example of this early in the book when the expected value was negative because the elementary error had been made of not considering doing nothing as one of the alternative actions. The situation was dealt with by incorporating 'dummy outcomes' into the analysis.

The process boils down to looking at the expected value or whatever criterion and saying 'that is not sufficiently high, what else can we do?'.

This attitude of creative thinking has nothing to do with decision theory and, ideally, should happen in any case. The best that can be said is that the formalism of the decision theory approach makes it slightly easier to see when new thinking is needed.

It must also be made clear that decision-theory methods can also lead to complacency. If the EV is adequately high (perhaps as a return on investment) then the project is inaugurated when a little more thought might have revealed a still better action. Dullness and lack of creativity are not caused by decision theory any more than their opposites but the result of the decision-theory analysis is a number which often seems to invest the analysis with a kind of intellectual and scientific respectability which may deaden further investigation. This phenomenon arises throughout managerial analysis, be it operational research, cost accounting, cash-flow analysis, or whatever. The calculations may be correct and based on tenable assumptions but have enough alternatives been looked at? The saving feature is that the formalism contained in these analyses makes the assumptions which have been made, and the alternatives which have been looked at, very plain but alert interpretation is still as valuable as ever it was without the aid of techniques.

Consistency

The manager called on to make a decision is faced with the difficult problem of ensuring that he is comparing like with like—in short, that he is being consistent in his judgements.

The difficulty is made more severe by the fact that he operates in an ever-changing world. In fact, much of what he does is directed towards bringing about the very changes which themselves make more difficult the choices which will lead to still more changes. For example, the manager who is trying to decide on an advertising campaign knows that it will affect in some way the pattern of demand and that will in turn affect the sales income which will influence his ability to make a success of the plant-expansion programme which he must also decide on. At the same time the plant expansion will provide the goods to sell to the market which will probably be generated by the advertising campaign. This is an involved cause-and-effect structure but it is the one within which he must operate. It does, however, make rationality and consistency harder to achieve.

Consistency does not mean uniformity. For example, if there are three plant sizes and three market sizes we could calculate pay offs and express them in a table as we have done before in this book. Armed with assessments of the probabilities for each market size we could then calculate expected value and, in principle, determine the optimal action to take now. There is a kind of disarming simplicity about all this which may lead to serious inconsistency.

In the examples in the book we assumed, for the sake of simplicity, that the probabilities of the outcomes were independent of the actions. For example, we made statements of the type 'there is a 30% probability of a small market, 40% of a medium market, and 30% of a large market'. Is it really consistent with reality to assume that these probabilities are not affected by the sizes of the plants which could be built? As always, it depends on the circumstances but the experienced reader will easily think of examples in which a large plant creates its own large market. This might well lead to a situation in which one had, instead of a simple list of probabilities, a table showing how the outcome probability was related to the action. For instance one could have:

		Small	*Medium*	*Large*
		\multicolumn{3}{c}{*Probability that the outcome will be a market size of*}		
Action Build	Small plant	0·50	0·30	0·20
	Medium plant	0·30	0·40	0·30
	Large plant	0·20	0·40	0·40

In this table, only the middle line is the same as the original statement about the probabilities of the various outcomes. The upper and lower lines have been altered to reflect management's judgement that the probabilities depend, at least in part, on the actions taken.

Whether one should use the simple probability statement or the more complex one depends on the kind of cause-and-effect structure in which the decision is embedded. This is not the place to go into the analysis of such structures—a field of its own called system dynamics. We merely content ourselves with observing that the problem exists and noting that one aspect of consistency is consistency with external reality. About the best that can be said is that the formalism and clarity of assumption inherent in decision theory at least make it easier to assess whether a particular analysis involved the appropriate assumptions. Decision theory certainly does not make the right assumptions.

The other aspect of consistency is that of consistency of assumptions from one problem to the next. Now, there is no reason why the assumptions have to be the same; we merely require that they be consistent with what was done in another problem, the experience which has been gained since, and any external changes there might have been. Decision theory can offer two lots of help in this, the clarity of assumption which we have already dealt with at some length and Bayes' theorem to which we devoted an earlier chapter.

Specialist techniques

Probably the least important of the attributes of decision theory in contributing to better management is its content of specialist techniques. As we have seen these include a variety of methods for finding optimal actions under varying circumstances and by different criteria. There are also methods such as Bayes' theorem and utility theory which are stages in the calculation. Clearly, a knowledge of an optimal course of action is nothing to be sneezed at and one would not assert that the techniques are unimportant, especially at the end of a book devoted to explaining them and dealing with the advantages of using them. Compared, however, to the advantages of having a *framework* for dealing with the widespread and serious difficulties of uncertainty, the benefits of clarity of assumption, comprehensiveness and consistency, the particular arithmetical methods have to be seen almost as a kind of incidental bonus. Perhaps the unfortunate feature of them is that the manager who wishes to obtain, in full, the other benefits must also expend some effort in mastering the techniques. It is certainly not sufficient, for reasons to be discussed later in this chapter, for the manager to say that he can always use a specialist and need not understand the methods himself. He must go to the trouble of acquiring at least the elementary skills for himself.

Having expatiated at this length about the virtues of decision theory, with only minor references to its snags, we ought now to redress the balance a little and point out the difficulties in rather more detail.

9.3 The problem of repeatability

A good slice of decision theory rests on the theory of probability. This in turn relies on a definition of 'probability' which is linked to the idea of repeatability as we explained in Chapter 2. A good many of the business decisions to which we are suggesting that decision theory should be applied are simply non-repeatable so how do we justify ourselves?

The answer lies in two ideas, neither of which is really sufficient in itself, but which, when taken together, provide a sufficient justification *in most cases*.

The ideas are, that repeatability is more a matter of similarity than actual identity, and the second, that if we do not use probability theory we have no other way of dealing with problems involving uncertainty.

Similarity and identity

We introduced the idea of repeatability by an example based on the performance of a large number of cars similar in make and age. Now, really, each of these cars is unique. They have different histories, have been driven and maintained with varying degrees of care, and each one either breaks down or it does not. Furthermore, a breakdown can be from one of many causes even if all the breakdowns involved the same component (which they would not). In fact, each car's history prior to and during the test is peculiar to itself yet we group them all together and use the results to generalize about other cars of similar type and history. Subject to one or two safeguards this is a perfectly respectable statistical procedure because it is recognized that the cars do not have to be identical but merely have enough common characteristics to be regarded as identical for the purpose in hand.

The same idea applies to business projects. They have the common characteristics of investments and money and can, therefore, be lumped together for purposes involving decision about investments and money. It is thus not too hard to justify the use of repeatability for the I.C.I.'s and General Motors' of this world because they are involved in such a continuing stream of projects that it is natural to use some idea of grouping and probability of outcome. At first sight the smaller firm may appear to be in a more difficult position because they initiate so few projects that repeatability is hard to envisage, let alone justify.

Two points may be made. First, a project does not have to involve vast resources to qualify for the application of decision theory, in fact, as we shall argue below it may be inappropriate to use it for the very largest projects of all. Even a small firm could well benefit from using decision theory for the many small (but large for it) projects in which it is involved. Second, even the small firm operates in a world in which there are many other projects and decisions going on—nearly all started by other firms, maybe in quite different industries, but all held together by the common threads of money and uncertainty.

Need to cope with uncertainty

About the only thing certain about the business world is that it is uncertain. Projects of all kinds succeed to unexpected degrees or even fail, markets grow or decline, machines perform as expected or they do not, marketing actions succeed to unpredictably varying extents, and so on, in endless variety.

The manager is faced with decision-making in this world and unless he is extremely innocent or very tough-minded he cannot ignore uncertainty and plough ahead as though the future were assured.

In view of these two considerations of similarity, rather than identity, and the need to cope in some way with uncertainty the most reasonable conclusion is that decision theory offers some help but its results must be assessed as carefully as those from any other form of analysis. It must also be pointed out that there are cases where the basic assumptions needed for the application of decision theory simply cannot be made. The manager using the theory must be alert for these instances but we can offer him little guidance on how to recognize them nor on what to do when he encounters one.

We now turn from general matters to some of the specific points in applying decision theory in practice.

9.4 Mental outlook

We have said that among the advantages of decision theory are that it provides for specific treatment of uncertainty. We have also said that, as we live in a world which is manifestly full of uncertainty, then we should attempt to take advantage of it in analysing the decisions we take. Experience of teaching managers confirms that these points are readily appreciated by practising managers and decision theory certainly goes down well with such groups.

At the same time there is a psychological disadvantage about admitting the possibility of failure in a project, or even thinking about the fact that it may be attended by varying degrees of success. There is something appealing about being able to say that the expected return on this investment will be $x\%$. Equally, there is the drawback that incorporating probabilities into the analysis does allow the excuse that failure was due to the way the chances turned out and not to lack of effort, skill, or judgement on the part of the people concerned. Clearly, we are faced with the impasse of the advantages of being able to incorporate uncertainty into the analysis, and the weaknesses attendant on doing so. If it is unrealistic to say that the uncertainties should be ignored and we should reject the methods of analysis described in this book it is equally unrealistic to pretend that the snags do not exist and to advocate the wholehearted and uncritical adoption of decision theory in all managerial decisions.

It seems to be generally the case that the adoption of improved methods of management carries with it the additional burden of ensuring that they are made to work properly. This was found out many years ago when the use of work-measurement techniques for setting labour targets was said to lead to a reduction in the authority and job satisfaction of first-line supervisors. That this was undoubtedly true was due to the uncritical acceptance of these new techniques as a substitute for the manager's real job of managing people. This was not necessarily the result of naïvety on the part of the managers; indeed, the situation was not helped by overselling on the part of practitioners and writers. The same kind of situation has arisen again and again in regard to the use of all the latest techniques from standard costing to management by exception and from network analysis to linear programming.

Obviously, what is needed is the attitude of mind which appreciates the advantages of improved decision analysis but is aware of the associated drawbacks. Unfortunately, it is a good deal easier to write a book describing theory and examples of applications than to explain how this desirable attitude of mind can be achieved. The variety of situations which can arise makes it impossible to do more than mention the problem. On the other side of the coin, the experience of managers in their day-to-day business of managing, motivating, and influencing others makes it unnecessary, and even presumptuous, to do more than mention that the problem exists.

9.5 Assessing probabilities

With only a few exceptions the techniques of decision theory call for the assessment of the probabilities to be attached to the various outcomes which will result from an action. This is frequently a point of great practical and psychological difficulty and we must provide at least some guide-lines to overcoming the difficulties.

One of the principal sources of difficulty is the manager who, when asked to assess the probabilities that, say, a market will rise, remain steady, or decline by particular amounts answers that he simply does not know and is therefore not willing to make any probability statement at all. Now, this man is faced with real difficulties and is not necessarily simply being uncooperative (we assume that he is a man whose responsibilities involve dealing with the market and that we have not asked the maintenance engineer who could quite legitimately have no idea at all about the market). The marketing manager knows perfectly well that markets are affected by many factors, some of which he does not even know about. It is, therefore, genuinely hard for him to assess what is likely to happen, especially when he is asked to talk about a range of possibilities. On the other hand, the marketing manager (and we are only using him as an illustration—these remarks apply to anyone else) is not being asked to make a probability assessment in a vacuum—he is continually faced with the decision of what to do about the market situation. This is not to imply that he is forever thinking about launching new products, stimulating demand for old ones, or redeploying his sales force. On the contrary, such things happen relatively infrequently and he may simply let things run as they are. That, however, is as much a decision as any other and is, in fact, precisely the 'do nothing' action which we discussed in Chapter 3. Now, if we assume that the marketing plan for the year is soundly based, it may well be right to do nothing if the market is not expected to deviate from the predicted path, in, say, the third quarter of the year. However, if the market is expected to rise, opportunities will be missed if nothing is done and it would be a rash man who did nothing about a falling market (we are assuming that the dynamics of the corporate system are such as to allow things to be done). Our manager has now got himself into the awkward position of taking a decision, even if it is only the implied one of doing nothing, in an environment in which he is not prepared to make statements about what the relative likelihood of the various outcomes might be. To be frank, he is blundering ahead into an uncertain future in the hope that things will turn out right in the end. Certainly, he has genuine difficulties in assessing the probabilities but the facts of the decision-orientated but uncertain environment in which he is placed positively require him to overcome these difficulties and assess the probabilities. This is easier said than done and we return to the topic below.

We must now digress to deal with the case of the manager who says, perhaps on the basis of detailed study, that the market demand will be, say, 120 units over the next 3 months instead of the previously expected 100 units. We have already said that the world is uncertain and, in most companies, a forecast like this would be treated with some reserve. Certainly, no statistical forecasting technique is capable of such exactitude for they all involve bands of probability. We must also observe that if, by production and stocks, 120 units are made available over the next 3 months then, as long as the demand is at least 120 units, more or less that number will be sold. This will be true if the demand is 120 or if it is 220. Thus, sales of 120 against a forecast of 120 may look like very good forecasting but the result is practically meaningless. All that can be said is that the forecast was not too low. This is a complicated matter into which we will not go deeper. We merely say that it is unrealistic to make exact forecasts and incorrect to use actual outcomes as a demonstration of forecasting accuracy. Our manager, whether he be a marketing man or has some other responsibilities, is forced to make probability statements and we now return to the question of helping him to do it.

There are basically three groups of techniques available—own opinion, group opinion, and statistical analysis. Most practical applications involve all three.

Own opinion
This is the simplest, in many ways the most appropriate, and at the same time potentially the most misleading method. The decision-maker simply writes down, using his own judgement, the probabilities he feels best suit the situation. The simplicity is obvious and the appropriateness comes from

the assessment being made by someone who is in touch with the situation and who will have to live with the consequences.

The disadvantages are that the manager may be called on to assess probabilities for a situation in which he has no basis of experience or knowledge on which to form an opinion and yet, for political reasons, be unable or unwilling to admit the fact. He may merely write down numbers in order to satisfy some rigmarole which he does not understand or sympathize with. His assessment is open to checking by other people and he may not be willing to play that game. Finally, although his eventual assumptions are open to view, his manner of reaching them cannot be checked or reviewed and is very hard to discuss.

Group opinion

This is really a refinement of the previous method in which, instead of one person assessing probabilities, a group of people do so. They may do this in committee or separately with their probabilities being 'averaged' in some way. This method has all the advantages and disadvantages of anything else which is done *en bloc*. Theoretically, one has access to a larger pool of experience but in practice the whole process is bedevilled by delay, subject to interpersonal political factors and, in the end, the responsibility is hard to pin down.

Statistical analysis

This is based on the idea that data from other decisions, market research, and opinion surveys such as those done by The Confederation of British Industry and other bodies can be used to work out the probabilities. For example, one might look at a large number of new product introductions, calculate the percentage in which demand was low, medium, or high, and use these figures to reflect the probabilities of the same market states in a forthcoming product launch.

The method has the advantage of appearing to be scientific in that the probabilities can be calculated exactly and unambiguously from given data and two analysts using the same data should reach the same conclusion. Unfortunately, exactness and lack of ambiguity may have nothing to do with relevance to the problem in hand. The argument is thus transferred from the probabilities to whether the data means anything—in other words, 'are we comparing like with like?'. This is not very useful because the argument should be about the probabilities themselves and it is merely fogging the issue to discuss something else.

The statistical methods have a place, it is true, but it is a rather limited one.

Of all these methods the one to be preferred in most cases is the first, providing it is coupled to a proper sensitivity analysis. This will reveal the probabilities to which the decision is particularly sensitive and then the second and third methods can be used, with due care, to assess the proper values to be used. The reader should think about why we use the term 'proper' values rather than 'accurate' or 'correct', in view of the discussion elsewhere in the book about repeatability and uniqueness.

9.6 Very large projects

We remarked earlier in this chapter that decision theory should not always be applied broadcast to all problems and that certain cases called for special treatment. The most obvious of these cases is the project which is very large in relation to the company's usual scale of decisions. Examples are, the opening of a major new plant, an acquisition or a merger, or a branching out into a whole new area of business. Typically, this kind of undertaking involves a decision to go ahead, or not, and then a whole series of smaller decisions are needed to ensure that the major decision will turn out to be successful.

It seems likely that these very large projects or VLP's are not necessarily initiated on the basis of objective criteria. Certainly, one can, in theory, treat them in exactly the same way as we have treated problems in the preceding eight chapters of this book but in practice it might prove rather hard to formulate the overall problem and quantify some of its aspects. For instance, a merger may be undertaken to ensure survival in an increasingly competitive environment or even, to be frank, for reasons of power and prestige. Some of these factors are rather hard to admit to, let alone to define and quantify. What then, is the role of decision theory in VLP's if it is not to be used in the actual decision process?

The answer is that it can be used in the analysis of the subordinate decisions which make up the VLP. For example, the profitability of a new mine would be affected very markedly by the price level obtained for the product. Many of these prices are very unstable and are impossible to forecast over even a few years while the mine may have a working life of 30 years. It is, therefore, not much use to try to incorporate the probabilities of various price levels in the decision to invest but, once that decision has been made, it would be very useful to try to work out optimal production policies when a period of, say, low price is succeeded by one of high price. The decision-tree method is ideal for this purpose.

As another example, one might decide to start an R & D programme to develop a range of new products, without using decision theory, because the problem is so unclear. One could then make use of Bayes' theorem to analyse the data on the likelihood of success for the various products as the R & D programme progresses.

In short, we must say that decision theory is even more of an aid *to* management than a substitute *for* management in the very large project than is normally the case.

9.7 Use specialists or do it yourself?

The reader who has got this far deserves our congratulations and is probably to be forgiven if he feels that there is no need to master all this himself as he can always use a specialist. Whilst this attitude is understandable it is also wrong. There are four principal reasons why the manager, who feels that decision theory has practical value in his firm, *must* acquire at least a basic working knowledge of what it is and how it is done.

Understanding the process

It is obviously true that the specialist in decision theory has a role to play in the firm which is using the methods. The functions of the expert in the theory include: (a) training, either formally or informally; (b) doing some of the donkey work in easy problems and making sure that the other people involved do their bits at the right time and in the proper way; and, (c) solving the more difficult problems.

Having admitted that, it must also be said that the manager cannot manage this process unless he has a fairly clear idea of what is going on. Furthermore, the manager will find it hard to control the process by asking the right questions, knowing what kind of answers to expect, and what they mean, unless he knows what is going on.

Confidential cases

The first reason does not necessarily mean that the manager has to know how to do the calculations, but the second reason does. This second reason is that there are some projects which, at least in their early stages, are so confidential or so apparently ridiculous and 'way out' that it might not do to involve someone else until the picture has been clarified somewhat. This will obviously involve the origination of the project in doing at least some of the easier arithmetic.

Attitude of mind

As well as certain arithmetical techniques, decision theory reflects an attitude of mind and a style of thinking. The most obvious examples are the decision tree and the theory of utility but the reader will have observed others. In many ways these habits of thought are more important than the arithmetical techniques as they can still provide a useful guide to action even when it is not possible to provide all the numbers required for a full-scale application of decision theory. Unfortunately, it is not easy to develop the mental attitude without also being able to do some of the calculations oneself.

Prestige

This final point may seem unimportant and irrational but the fact remains that it is not always appropriate for a senior manager to call in a specialist to do every little piece of arithmetic.

9.8 Changing the probabilities

Decision theory is all very well but it inevitably implies that the risks involved in a business decision are there to be taken and that the decision-maker merely has to make the best of them. Now, this is far from being the case and by far the best thing to do in an uncertain situation is to change the odds in ones own favour. If this can be done it is far more useful than calculating the expected value and then sitting back and waiting for events to take their course. At first sight this policy makes decision theory irrelevant, but a little thought will show that this is far from being the case. Let us consider a simple illustration.

A project has returns of -200, -100, or 400 depending on which of outcomes I, II, or III happen. It seems that $P(\text{I}) = 0 \cdot 20$, $P(\text{II}) = 0 \cdot 50$, and $P(\text{III}) = 0 \cdot 30$, thus, the expected value is $+30$. Let us assume that $+30$ is no great sum to the firm so the project is not really very attractive. Clearly, if $P(\text{III})$ could be raised to $0 \cdot 50$ while $P(\text{I})$ was driven to zero then the EV would become 150—an improvement of 120. If the cost of the advertising, product development, or whatever, needed to change the probabilities in this way can be compared with 120 then one has some idea of whether it is worth the effort to try to change the probabilities. This is the true meaning of sensitivity analysis. It is not merely a method of altering probabilities in a problem but of examining the problem *itself* to see what can be done, at what cost, and with what benefits. It is possible to make the sensitivity analysis very sophisticated by attaching probabilities to probabilities but that is beyond the scope of this book.

9.9 Conclusion

There are no problems in this chapter because the whole book is really a problem in itself—'what is decision theory, can I use it, if so what will I get out of it, and how can I set about employing these methods?'.

Appendix A

Proof that Bayes' strategies are the same for maximum EV and minimum EOL

Following this proof is not necessary to understand the book. It is not completely rigorous but it indicates the mode of proof.

Consider a pay off table for two actions and two outcomes with a, b, c, and d denoting the pay offs:

		Outcome		
		I	II	EV
Probability		P_1	P_2	
Action	A	a	b	$P_1a + P_2b$
	B	c	d	$P_1c + P_2d$

Suppose that

$$P_1a + P_2b > P_1c + P_2d \qquad (A.1)$$

so A is the Bayes' strategy.

From Eqn (A.1)

$$P_2(b - d) > P_1(c - a) \qquad (A.2)$$

To calculate the COL table assume

$$c > a \quad \text{and} \quad b > d$$

(Any other assumption will do.)

Then the COL table will be:

		Outcome		
		I	II	EOL
Probability		P_1	P_2	
Action	A	$c - a$	0	$P_1(c - a)$
	B	0	$b - d$	$P_2(b - d)$

From Eqn (A.2)

$$P_1(c - a) < P_2(b - d)$$

so using the minimum EOL criteria action A will be the Bayes strategy, as before. This completes the proof.

By making a particular set of assumptions about a, b, c, and d one can prove that maximin pay off and minimax opportunity loss always lead to the same strategy. Unfortunately, by making different assumptions about a, b, c, and d we get the result that the two criteria always give different results. This confirms that conflict or agreement between the non-Bayes criteria is purely a matter of the values in the table. The proof for the bayesian case always holds regardless of what is assumed about the pay off table.

Appendix B

Decision tree for the Heath Robinson Engineering Company

A suitable tree is shown in Fig. B.1. This is not the only tree which could

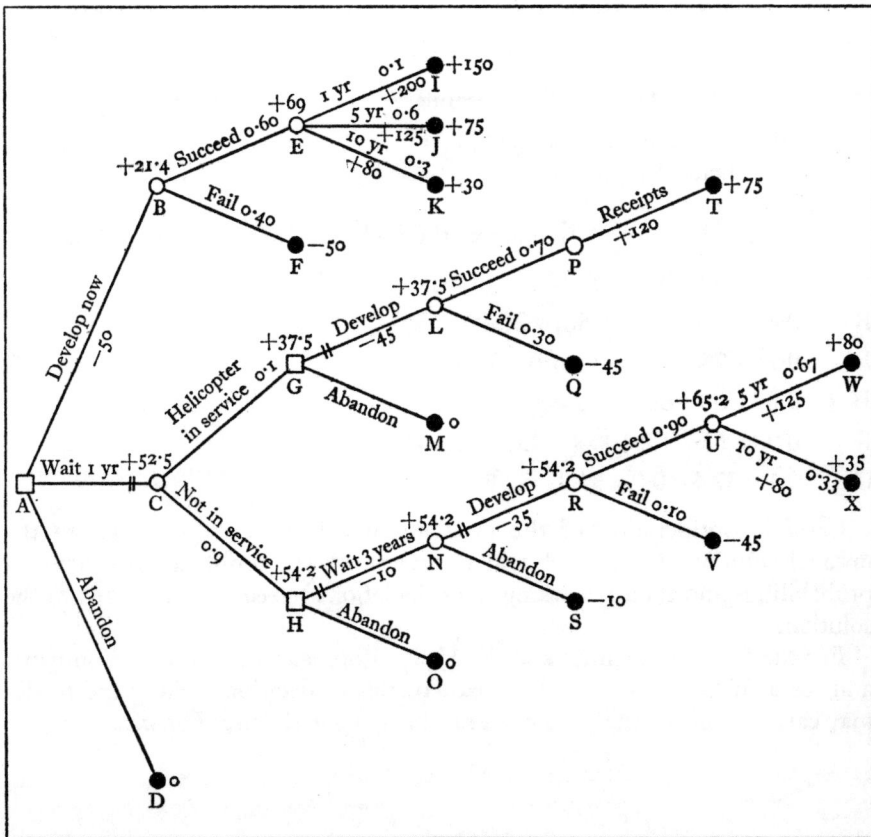

Fig. B.1 Decision tree for the Heath Robinson Engineering Company

be drawn and the reader should check his version against the diagram to see whether the end result is the same.

In the diagram the probabilities and the associated costs or revenues are written against the branch to which they apply. The cash flows have been added along the branches to give a resultant final figure which is written at the end of the branch. This resultant figure is carried back, weighted by the probabilities to determine the optimal branches.

This procedure is an alternative to the one described in the chapter where the cost or income for each step in chain was deducted or added as we came to it. The two procedures give identical results and the choice is a matter of preference.

The only place at which the probabilities need modifying from the values in the text is in the last part of the middle chain. After 1 year has passed the aircraft can only come into service at either 5 years or 10 years. On the data given the total probability is $0.6 + 0.3 = 0.9$. The individual values must add to 1.00 and this is achieved by scaling them up by dividing each by 0.9. This leads to

$$\frac{0.6}{0.9} = 0.67 \quad \text{and} \quad \frac{0.7}{0.9} = 0.33$$

and

$$0.67 + 0.33 = 1.00 \quad \text{as required}$$

The optimal branches are marked $||$. The notation '1 yr', '5 yr', and '10 yr' denotes the helicopter coming into service 1 year, 5 years, and 10 years from the present.

Expected values are written above the nodes and are calculated as follows.

E $0.1 \times 150 + 0.6 \times 75 + 0.3 \times 30 = 69$
B $0.6 \times 69 + 0.4 \times (-50) = 21.4$
L $0.70 \times 75 + 0.30 \times (-45) = 37.5$
U $0.67 \times 80 + 0.33 \times 35 = 65.2$
R $0.90 \times 65.2 + 0.10 \times (-45) = 54.2$
C $0.1 \times 37.4 + 0.9 \times 54.2 = 52.53$

Careful consideration of the problem may have led the reader to the optimal solution. If so he should try rewriting the problem with different probabilities and then reworking the calculations to see what happens to the solution.

For the further adventures of the Heath Robinson Engineering Company, and for a fuller coverage of the mathematics of decision-making the reader may care to consult the author's *Mathematics for Business Decisions*.

Solutions to problems

Chapter 1 Decision making

1. The lowest pay offs for each action are

A	10
B	-30
C	20

Note that action B can lead to a situation in which there are losses.

The largest of these smallest values is for action C which is, therefore, the maximin pay off action.

2. The COL table is

		Outcome		
		I	II	III
	A	30	10	35
Action	B	70	0	0
	C	0	0	40

(Note $40 - (-30) = 40 + 30$.)

The maximum opportunity losses for the actions are

A	35
B	70
C	40

The smallest of these is 35 so A is the minimax opportunity loss action.

3. The first point is that Action B is always at least as good as Action C. Usually it is rather better and would, therefore, always be chosen in preference to C which may then be eliminated.

The pay off table beomes

		Outcome				Minimum
		I	II	III	IV	pay off
	A	30	40	35	90	30
Action	B	60	30	40	30	30
	D	40	20	50	60	20

and the maximin pay off action is A or B.

The opportunity loss table is

		Outcome				Maximum
		I	II	III	IV	OL
	A	30	0	15	0	30
Action	B	0	10	10	60	60
	D	20	20	0	30	30

and the minimax OL is either A *or* D.

This is an example of a situation in which decision theory does not lead to a clear-cut recommendation to action. The implication in a practical case is that the original analysis was not refined enough to show up the differences between the two projects. It may be that the differences between the two projects are not quantifiable economically and the original pay off table is the best that can be done. The indication from decision theory in such a case is that the *economic* interest of the firm would be equally well served by either project, as long as minimax opportunity loss is the proper criterion to use. The firm is, therefore, genuinely in a position to select between A and D on the basis of non-economic criteria.

4. The first point is that these are all *costs* and the pay off table is:

	Ground clear	Ground obstructed	Minimum pay off
One small and one large	− 100	− 150	− 150
Two large	− 80	− 200	− 200

Using the maximin criterion the optimal act is to have one small and one large excavator.

The COL table turns out to be:

	Ground clear	Ground obstructed	Maximum OL
One small and one large	20	0	20
Two large	0	50	50

and the minimax opportunity loss criterion also gives one small and one large excavator as the optimal choice.

Notice that the negative signs have to be treated with some caution. In calculating the OL table − 80 is *greater* than − 100 because it is less negative. This leads to the calculation

$$-80 - (-100) = -80 + 100 = +20$$

for the COL for one small and one large excavator in unobstructed ground.

5. The pay off table (including the negative signs) is now:

		Ground state				Minimum pay off
		A	B	C	D	
	I	− 70	− 170	− 250	− 270	− 270
Equipment	II	− 150	− 160	− 200	− 230	− 230
combination	III	− 80	− 140	− 180	− 210	− 210
	IV	− 160	− 120	− 140	− 160	− 160

On the basis of maximin pay off the optimal equipment combination is IV—one large excavator, one small one, and the demolition equipment.

The Site Agent also calculates the opportunity loss table and finds the COL table:

		Ground state				Maximum OL
		A	B	C	D	
	I	0	50	110	110	110
Equipment	II	80	40	60	70	80
combination	III	10	20	40	30	40
	IV	90	0	0	0	90

The minimax opportunity loss is 40 indicating equipment combination III—two large excavators and the demolition equipment.

6. The most obvious managerial problems are:

(a) Conflict of evidence between experts. The cost figures are different and the alternatives are not the same.

(b) How does the manager ensure that enough alternatives have been examined?

(c) The very important fact that it is often not very useful to think about a project in terms of it 'succeeding' or 'failing'. There are many projects, particularly those involving engineering or scientific development but also those including some marketing problems, where the project can be made to work providing enough is spent on it. This is sometimes not explicitly stated but it is, in many cases, more useful to analyse the project, in terms of the cost of making it work rather than in terms of different outcomes from a project which is certain to work for a fixed investment.

Chapter 2 Probability

1.
$$P(D) = 1.00 - P(A) - P(B) - P(C) = 0.3$$
$$P(A \cup C) = 0.2 + 0.4 = 0.6$$
$$P(A \cup B) = 0.2 + 0.1 = 0.3$$
$$P(A \cup C \cup D) = 0.2 + 0.4 + 0.3 = 0.9$$
$$P(A \cup D) = 0.2 + 0.3 = 0.5$$
$$P(B \cup C \cup A) = P(A \cup B \cup C) = 0.2 + 0.1 + 0.4 = 0.7$$

2. The first part is to find

$$P(A|(A \cup C)) = \frac{P(A)}{P(A \cup C)} = \frac{0.2}{0.6} = 0.333$$

$$P(B|(B \cup A \cup D)) = \frac{0.1}{0.1 + 0.2 + 0.3} = 0.167$$

3.
$$P(A \cap B) = 0.2 \times 0.1 = 0.02$$
$$P(A \cap C \cap D) = 0.2 \times 0.4 \times 0.3 = 0.024$$
$$P(A \cap A) = 0.2 \times 0.2 = 0.04$$
$$P(A \cap A \cap B) = P(A \cap A) \times P(B) = 0.004$$
$$P(A \cap B \cap C \cap D) = 0.2 \times 0.1 \times 0.4 \times 0.3 = 0.0024$$

Care is needed with decimal points!

4. (a) Given that $P(Y|X) = 0.30$ and $P(X) = 0.60$

$$P(X \cap Y) = P(X) \ P(Y|X) \text{ from Eqn (2.2.)}$$

Hence $P(X \cap Y) = 0.6 \times 0.3 = 0.18$

(b) We are told that $P(X \cap Y) = 0.25$ while $P(Y|X)$ is still 0.30.

Applying Eqn 2.3 we find

$$P(X) = \frac{0.25}{0.30} = 0.835$$

(c) This implies that

$$P(X) = \frac{0.40}{0.30} = 1.33$$

Either someone's leg is being pulled or a mistake has been made. The moral is that probabilities are merely information and no more. Any information can be wrong and *all* information should be checked as far as possible using whatever means are open to you.

5. $P(A \cup B) = P(A) + P(B) - P(A \cap B)$

from equation 2·6.

Hence $P(A \cup B) = 0·4 + 0·3 - 0·4 \times 0·3 = 0·58$

            $P(B \cup C) = P(B) + P(C) - P(B \cap C)$

                     $= 0·3 + 0·2 - 0·3 \times 0·2$

                     $= 0·44$

$P(A \cup B \cup C)$ is rather harder but it turns out that

         $P(A \cup B \cup C) = P(A) + P(B) + P(C) - P(A \cap B) - P(B \cap C) -$

                                             $P(A \cap C) - 2 P(A \cap B \cap C).$

This can be seen by drawing three overlapping circles to represent A, B, and C thus:

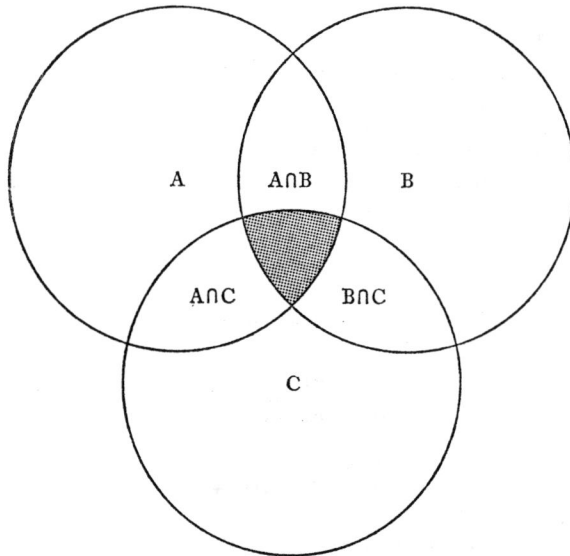

There are three segments where two circles overlap—denoted by $A \cap B$, $A \cap C$, and $B \cap C$. In the centre there is a small shaded area where all three overlap. This area represents $A \cap B \cap C$ and has to be subtracted twice because there are two overlaps. The other overlapping areas do so only once.

     Thus:

         $P(A \cup B \cup C) = 0·4 + 0·3 + 0·2 - 0·4 \times 0·3 - 0·4 \times 0·2$

                               $- 0·3 \times 0·2 - 2 \times 0·4 \times 0·3 \times 0·2$

                 $= 0·9 - 0·12 - 0·08 - 0·06 - 0·048$

                 $= 0·592$

This means that there is a 59·2 % chance that any one of A, B, or C will occur.

Chapter 3   Bayes' strategies

1. The expected value is

         $0·40 \times 25 - 0·20 \times 40 + 0·20 \times 16 - 0·20 \times 8$

           $= 10 - 8 + 3·2 - 1·6$

           $= 3·6$

2 The answer is 0·32 (to two places of decimals). This gives an EV of

         $0·40 \times 25 - 0·20 \times 40 + 0·32 \times 16 - 0·08 \times 80$

           $= 10 - 8 + 5·12 - 6·4$

           $= 0·72$

There are two ways of doing this. First note that since the probabilities for outcomes I and II have been fixed and total 0·6 those for III and IV must also total 0·4.

This means that if the probability of outcome III is p that of outcome IV has to be $(0·4 - p)$ and p must not be larger than 0·4. (Why?)

We then have the expected value as

$$0·40 \times 25 - 0·20 \times 16 + p \times 0·40 \times 25 - 0·20$$
$$\times 40 + p \times 16 - (0·4 - p) \times 80$$

and a process of trial and error leads to $p = 0·32$ having a small positive pay off.

Another way is to find the value of p which makes the expected value just zero and then rounding it up to two decimal places. This leads to

$$0·40 \times 25 - 0·20 \times 40 + p \times 16 - (0·40 - p) \times 80 = 0$$

or

$$10 - 8 + 16p - 32 + 80p = 0$$

so

$$96p = 30$$

or

$$p = 30/96 = 0·313$$

so $p = 0·32$ makes the project slightly profitable.

3. The main implication is that there is nothing sacrosanct about probabilities. The solution may change markedly for fairly small changes in the probabilities so it is a good idea to do some test calculations showing how the solution would change if the given probabilities were altered slightly.

Bear in mind that a statement about probability is neither proved or disproved by the occurrence (or non-occurrence) of the event to which it refers. It is only when the event is repeatable that, in a suitably long run, we can measure the probability of the event taking place.

4. This problem has a slight catch in it, designed to show the virtue of common sense applied to decision theory. Action A always leads to a worse pay off than action B no matter what the outcome is. In the circumstances we would always avoid action A so that we can drop it from further consideration. This leaves the pay off table having only two rows and

$$\begin{aligned} EV(B) &= 70 \times 0·40 + 95 \times 0·20 + 165 \times 0·30 + 120 \times 0·10 \\ &= 28 + 19 + 49·5 + 12 \\ &= 108·5 \end{aligned}$$

$$\begin{aligned} EV(C) &= 90 \times 0·40 + 80 \times 0·20 + 190 \times 0·30 + 70 \times 0·10 \\ &= 36 + 16 + 57 + 7 \\ &= 116 \end{aligned}$$

It is fairly evident from the table that action C is likely to be optimal because it has a higher pay off than B for outcomes I and III where the probabilities are high and a pay off for outcomes II and IV which is not a lot lower. By calculation it turns out that the difference in expected value is rather small (about 7 %) so that in practice we should probably feel that there was little to choose between the two actions.

The COL table becomes:

		Outcome			
		I	II	III	IV
Action	B	20	0	25	0
	C	0	15	0	50

and

$$\begin{aligned} EOL(B) &= 20 \times 0·40 + 0 \times 0·20 + 25 \times 0·30 + 0 \times 0·10 \\ &= 8 + 7·5 = 15·5 \end{aligned}$$

H<small>DA</small>

$$\text{EOL(C)} = 0 \times 0.40 + 15 \times 0.20 + 0 \times 0.30 + 50 \times 0.10$$
$$= 3 + 5 = 8$$

Action C has the lower EOL and would therefore be chosen. Notice that $15.5 - 8 = 7.5$, which was the difference in EV, and also that action C remains optimal when the criterion is changed from maximum EV to minimum EOL. This is precisely the point made in the chapter.

5. There is a lot of arithmetic and discussion in this problem. The arithmetic is the same as before but remember that the outcomes are collectively exhaustive and mutually exclusive.

6. The pay off table was

		Outcome			Expected
		I	II	III	value
Probability		0·4	0·2	0·4	
	A	10	20	25	18
Action	B	− 30	30	60	18
	C	40	30	20	30

The maximum EV is for action C.

7. The new calculation is

		Outcome			Expected
		I	II	III	value
Probability		0·5	0·4	0·1	
	A	10	20	25	15·5
Action	B	− 30	30	60	3
	C	40	30	20	34

Notice that although the expected values for Actions A, B, and C have all been altered, the result remains the same in that action C is still the Bayes Strategy. In this sense the problem is insensitive to that particular change in the probabilities. Would it be completely insensitive to probability changes?

Chapter 5 Utility

1. Recalling that all the figures were costs we had the pay off table:

	Ground clear	Ground obstructed
One small and one large machine	− 100	− 150
Two large machines	− 80	− 200

The utility values are found simply by reading from the graph and are
$$-£80\,000 = -14 \text{ U}$$
$$-£100\,000 = -20 \text{ U}$$
$$-£150\,000 = -44 \text{ U}$$
$$-£200\,000 = -100 \text{ U}$$

This leads to the utility table:

	Clear	Obstructed	Minimum
One small and one large	− 20	− 44	− 44
Two large	− 14	− 100	− 100

So the maximin utility strategy is still to have one large and one small machine.

We can calculate the conditional utility losses exactly as for conditional opportunity losses and the result is:

Conditional utility loss	Ground clear	Ground obstructed	Maximum
One small and one large	6	0	6
Two large	0	56	56

The minimax utility loss strategy is, again, one small and one large machine.

2. The first stage is simply to read off from the graph the appropriate utility values. For Problem 1 of Chapter 3 this leads to

$$£25\,000 = 2\!\cdot\!2 \text{ U}$$
$$-£40\,000 = -5\!\cdot\!5 \text{ U}$$
$$£16\,000 = 1\!\cdot\!5 \text{ U}$$
$$-£8\,000 = -0\!\cdot\!9 \text{ U}$$

The expected utility is

$$0\!\cdot\!40 \times 2\!\cdot\!2 - 0\!\cdot\!20 \times 5\!\cdot\!5 + 0\!\cdot\!20 \times 1\!\cdot\!5 - 0\!\cdot\!20 \times 0\!\cdot\!9$$
$$= 0\!\cdot\!88 - 1\!\cdot\!10 + 0\!\cdot\!30 - 0\!\cdot\!18$$
$$= -0\!\cdot\!10$$

This is in flat contradiction to the result found by computing expected value.

The second half of the problem is done in much the same way. Action A can still be dropped from consideration as a moment's thought will show.

Reading from the graph we obtain the table:

		Outcome			
		I	II	III	IV
Probability		0·40	0·20	0·30	0·10
Action	B	7·0	8·5	13·5	10·5
	C	8·0	7·2	14·5	7·0

We now have

$$\text{EV(B)} = 0\!\cdot\!40 \times 7\!\cdot\!0 + 0\!\cdot\!20 \times 8\!\cdot\!5 + 0\!\cdot\!30 \times 13\!\cdot\!5 + 0\!\cdot\!10 \times 10\!\cdot\!5$$
$$= 2\!\cdot\!80 + 1\!\cdot\!70 + 4\!\cdot\!05 + 1\!\cdot\!05$$
$$= 9\!\cdot\!60$$

$$\text{EV(C)} = 0\!\cdot\!40 \times 8\!\cdot\!0 + 0\!\cdot\!20 \times 7\!\cdot\!2 + 0\!\cdot\!30 \times 14\!\cdot\!5 + 0\!\cdot\!10 \times 7\!\cdot\!0$$
$$= 3\!\cdot\!20 + 1\!\cdot\!44 + 4\!\cdot\!35 + 0\!\cdot\!70$$
$$= 9\!\cdot\!69$$

Notice that in this case action C is still to be preferred to action B, as it was under the criterion of expected monetary value. The point of using utility is that it more accurately reflects the fact that the two actions are very finely balanced. Under EMV the difference was about 7 %, now it is less than 1 %. The advantage of knowing that the two actions are virtually equivalent is not that we should now toss a coin to choose between them but, that they should be re-examined to see whether we have properly evaluated them in the first place. The prompting for the re-examination comes from the decision-theory analysis because the equivalence of two projects is far from evident when one looks at the original table of pay offs. It is one of the side benefits of a formal use of decision theory that it forces assumptions and data into the open for very close examination.

3. We know that $£400\,000 = 3$ U and, of course that $£0 = 0$ U.

Let X be the utility value for $-£400\,000$. We know that, for the decision-maker to be indifferent about a project with pay offs of $£400\,000$ and $-£400\,000$ and a $0\cdot625$ probability of getting the larger pay off that, in utility,

$$3 \times 0\!\cdot\!625 + X \times (1 - 0\!\cdot\!625) = 0$$
$$X = \frac{-3 \times 0\!\cdot\!625}{0\!\cdot\!375} = -5$$

*HDA

For a deal involving pay offs of $-£200000$ and $+£400000$ with a success probability of 0·400 we have, again putting X for the utility of $-£200000$

$$3 \times 0.400 + X \times (1 - 0.400) = 0$$

so

$$X = \frac{-3 \times 0.400}{0.600} = -2$$

Similarly, for a deal involving $£200000$ and $-£200000$ we find that according to the Heath Robinson Engineering Company, the utility of $£200000$ is 1.

These points should be plotted on a graph, and a curve drawn through them will be the Heath Robinson Engineering Company's utility curve.

5. The curve passes through the points

Pay off (£)	Utility
− 100 000	− 70
− 50 000	− 20
0	0
100 000	10
200 000	15
300 000	17·5
400 000	20

The shape is strongly risk-averse

Chapter 6 Bayes' theorem

1. This is solved very simply by using the methods of the chapter. The calculation proceeds by first calculating the joint probabilities for the three states of the process and the effect D. This is done by multiplying the figures in the column for D by the corresponding values for the state of the process.

Cause (process state)	Original probability for that cause	Probability of poor batch for each cause	Col (2) × Col (3) = joint probability of cause and effect
A	0·2	0·7	0·14
B	0·6	0·2	0·12
C	0·2	0·1	0·02
		Total	0·28

Then, using the Bayes' formula as in Section 6.2

$$P(A|D) = \frac{0.14}{0.28} = 0.50$$

$$P(B|D) = \frac{0.12}{0.28} = 0.43$$

$$P(C|D) = \frac{0.02}{0.28} = 0.07$$

Thus, given the information that the batch was poor the conditional probabilities are that

Process is running	Revised probability
Badly (A)	0·50
Adequately (B)	0·43
Well (C)	0·07

These may be compared with the original probabilities of 0·2, 0·6, and 0·2 respectively.

2. Before the batch was tested the probabilities were

$$P(A) = 0·2$$
$$P(B) = 0·6$$
$$P(C) = 0·2$$

EV of adjusting the process $= 0·8 \times -400 + 0·2 \times 300$
$$= -260$$

EV of leaving it alone $\quad = 0·2 \times -300 + 0·8 \times 0$
$$= -60$$

The optimal act is to leave the process alone.
After the batch is found to be faulty

EV of adjusting $\quad = 0·5 \times -400 + 0·5 \times 300$
$$= -50$$

EV of leaving it alone $= 0·5 \times -300 + 0·5 \times 0$
$$= -150$$

The optimal act is now to adjust the process.

This problem is a very simple example of how the results of the prior/posterior analysis can be fed into a decision analysis. Clearly the probabilities which come out of the prior/posterior analysis can be used in any of the methods discussed in this book.

3. We proceed in the same way as in the Chapter. It is really only necessary to do the calculation for column III of the probability table, but we shall do it all for completeness.

		Prior probability	Conditional probability for effects			Joint probability for effects		
			I	II	III	I	II	III
	A	0·20	0·60	0·30	0·10	0·12	0·06	0·02
Cause	B	0·30	0·40	0·40	0·20	0·12	0·12	0·06
	C	0·50	0·20	0·30	0·50	0·10	0·15	0·25
						0·34	0·33	0·33

$$P(A \mid III) = \frac{0·02}{0·33} = 0·06$$

$$P(B \mid III) = \frac{0·06}{0·33} = 0·18$$

$$P(C \mid III) = \frac{0·25}{0·33} = 0·76$$

The probabilities asked for in the question are 76%, 18%, and 6% for 'expand', 'maintain' and 'reduce' respectively compared with the original values of 50%, 30%, and 20%.

If advertising had stayed at the existing level the probabilities would have been 46%, 36%, and 18%. If advertising had fallen the values would have been 30%, 35%, and 35% respectively.

4. The solution is in the chapter.

5. The calculation can be simplified somewhat by using the knowledge that we only need deal with the sequence, high, medium, high. This means that instead of calculating all the joint-probability table we need only the column for the event which occurred. This also means that we need use only the column of the conditional-probability table for the event we have to deal with. The resulting calculation takes about 10 minutes and can be laid out in the following way.

Month 1   Enquiries were high

		Prior probabilities for			Conditional probability for	Joint probabilities of high for		
		O	N	P	high	O	N	P
	B	0·10	0·30	0·70	0·10	0·01	0·03	0·07
State	I	0·20	0·40	0·20	0·20	0·04	0·08	0·04
	G	0·70	0·30	0·10	0·60	0·42	0·18	0·06
		1·00	1·00	1·00		0·47	0·29	0·17

Dividing the entries in the columns of the joint-probability end of the table by the column totals leads to the posterior distributions for month 1 which become the priors for month 2.

Month 2   Enquiries were low

		Prior probabilities for			Conditional probability for	Joint probabilities of low for		
		O	N	P	low	O	N	P
	B	0·021	0·103	0·412	0·80	0·017	0·082	0·330
State	I	0·085	0·276	0·235	0·20	0·017	0·055	0·047
	G	0·894	0·621	0·353	0·10	0·089	0·062	0·035
		1·000	1·000	1·000		0·123	0·199	0·412

Notice the way in which errors due to rounding-off can creep in. The respective joint-probabilities for O and B, and O and I were 0·01 and 0·04 in the first table and these are now converted into the new prior probabilities assigned by O to B and I—the top two entries in the extreme left-hand column in the table for month 2. Since 0·04 is four times 0·01 we should have expected the entries in the month 2 table also to be in the ratio of 4 to 1. In fact, they are 0·085 and 0·021 which is not quite 4 to 1. This is due to carrying out the calculation to three decimal places. It could be done to four or more decimal places but that would need a calculating machine. In this case the difference is very slight and can be ignored but care has to be exercised. This kind of phenomenon shows the advantage of having a computer program if one is to apply decision theory on any material scale. Such a program can be written to contain powerful checks against the accumulation of rounding errors.

Returning to the problem, we now calculate the posterior distribution at the end of month 2 and make it the prior for month 3. As before we take the values from the three right-hand columns of the month 2 table and divide by the respective column totals. We adjust, where necessary, in the third decimal place to make the total for the new priors come to 1·00. We obtain:

Month 3   Enquiries were high

		Prior probabilities for			Conditional probability for	Joint probabilities of high for		
		O	N	P	high	O	N	P
	B	0·138	0·412	0·801	0·10	0·014	0·041	0.080
State	I	0·138	0·276	0·114	0·20	0·028	0·055	0·023
	G	0·724	0·312	0·085	0·60	0·434	0·187	0·051
		1·000	1·000	1·000		0·476	0·283	0·154

From the right-hand column we calculate the posterior at the end of the third month and obtain:

		Posterior for		
		O	N	P
	B	0·029	0·145	0·520
State	I	0·059	0·194	0·149
	G	0·912	0·661	0·331
		1·000	1·000	1·000

We now summarize the calculation by tabulating the distributions for the three decision-makers at each of the four stages in the project—the start and the ends of each of the 3 months.

		Start			End of								
					Month 1			Month 2			Month 3		
		O	N	P	O	N	P	O	N	P	O	N	P
	B	0·10	0·30	0·70	0·021	0·103	0·414	0·138	0·412	0·801	0·029	0·145	0·520
State	I	0·20	0·40	0·30	0·085	0·276	0·235	0·138	0·276	0·114	0·059	0·194	0·149
	G	0·70	0·30	0·10	0·894	0·621	0·353	0·724	0·312	0·085	0·912	0·661	0·331

Clearly, there has been nothing like the convergence of opinion that there was in the chapter example. This is hardly surprising as the evidence is by no means as clear cut especially when viewed from the starting points of the three participants. In this way, Bayes' theorem gives results which are very much in accord with real life. The advantage of the theorem is that it incorporates growing experience in a coherent, consistent fashion—a result which is rarely possible in debate and discussion.

The main value of the bayesian approach lies not in the calculation of revised probabilities but in the way in which the revised probabilities can be used to calculate EMV or EV. In this example, the calculation of EMV, say, could decide whether the project should be continued or not.

Chapter 7 The economics of information

1. First convert the pay off table to conditional opportunity losses.
COL table

		Outcome			
		I	II	III	EOL
Probability		0·4	0·2	0·4	
Action	C	0	0	40	16

We need only the last row as we already know, from problem 4 of Chapter 3, that C is the action for maximum EV and we also know that this action will also give the minimum EOL. Since the EOL for Action C is 16 this is the EVPI.

2. Convert to a COL table and calculate the EOL.

COL table

		Outcome				
		I	II	III	IV	EOL
Probability		0·2	0·4	0·3	0·1	
	A	10	0	30	0	8·0
Action	B	0	30	0	55	17·5
	C	5	20	10	75	19·5

The optimal act is A with a minimum EOL of 8·0 and this is the EVPI.

3. The working for a forecast of outcome I is shown in detail and the others in summary form. The forecast error is distributed evenly over the other 3 outcomes.

COL table

		Outcome				
		I	II	III	IV	EOL
Probability		0·85	0·05	0·05	0·05	
	A	10	0	30	0	10·00
Action	B	0	30	0	55	4·25
	C	5	20	10	75	9·50

The optimal act is, as would be expected, B with an EOLI(I) of 4·25.
The other EOLIs are

$$\text{EOLI(II)} = 2·00$$
$$\text{EOLI(III)} = 4·25$$
$$\text{EOLI (IV)} = 2·00$$

The overall EOLI is found from these values by multiplying by the original probabilities and adding (review the arguments in the text). The result is that EOLI = 3·125. The reduction in EOL brought about by the information, i.e., the EVSI is

$$\text{EVSI} = \text{EVPI} - \text{EOLI}$$
$$= 8·0 - 3·125 = 4·875.$$

Since the cost of the information is 3 and its value is nearly 5 in theory the information is worth buying. Using the 'half-EVSI' rule it would not be.

4. The first thing to notice is that action D should be ignored because it is always worse than action C (D is said to be 'dominated' by C). We thus have a pay off table of:

		Outcome			
		I	II	III	IV
Probability		0·10	0·20	0·50	0·20
	A	20	60	70	190
Action	B	40	30	90	20
	C	110	100	40	130

The problem can be solved using expected values but it is less laborious to go to opportunity losses.

COL table

		Outcome			
		I	II	III	IV
Probability		0·10	0·20	0·50	0·20
	A	90	100	20	0
Action	B	70	130	0	170
	C	0	0	50	40

and, as before, we find

$$\text{EOL(A)} = 39$$
$$\text{EOL(B)} = 67$$
$$\text{EOL(C)} = 33$$

Action C has the minimum EOL so, recalling the discussion in the chapter, the EVPI is also 33.

When the probabilities are reversed we would have:

COL table

		Outcome			
		I	II	III	IV
Probability		0·20	0·50	0·20	0·10
	A	90	100	20	0
Action	B	70	130	0	170
	C	0	0	50	40

and

$$EOI(A) = 78$$
$$EOL(B) = 96$$
$$EOL(C) = 14$$

Notice that the choice of action has not altered and remains at C. However, the minimum EOL is now only 14 and the answer to the second numerical part of the question is that the EVPI is now 14.

The main managerial implication is that the assessment of probabilities has some curious effects, hence the importance of a proper sensitivity analysis. In this case the optimal action is not changed but the economics of the problem change very much (work out the expected values). In other cases the optimal action might be altered by varying the probabilities.

Notice that sensitivity analysis (i.e., seeing how sensitive the answer is to changes in the data) is a subject in its own right. In this case we reversed the order of the probabilities which, on the face of it, seems fairly sweeping. In fact, it is not because the pay offs from action C are very large for outcomes I, II, and IV and reversing the probabilities makes little real difference for outcomes I and IV. One must, in fact, examine the pattern of outcomes and pay offs before doing a sensitivity analysis. In this case, action C practically selects itself unless the probabilities are very heavily concentrated on outcome II or IV. In short, the arithmetic is very useful, but it has to be used with a good dose of common sense and insight into the problem.

5. The calculations appear to be a little tedious but can be done fairly rapidly once the data are available and with a little practice. Again a pre-written standard computer program would make the labour trivial compared to the managerial benefit of the information, let alone its economic value.

We proceed by dealing with each of the four outcomes which could be forecast calculating the EOLI for each. The first step is to calculate the revised outcome probabilities.

Outcome I forecast

We know from the problem statement that the probabilities are:

Outcome	Probability
I	0·80
II	0·175
III	0·050
IV	0·025

so the EOLI would be found from:

COL table

		Outcome			
		I	II	III	IV
Probability		0·80	0·125	0·05	0·025
	A	90	100	20	0
Action	B	70	130	0	170
	C	0	0	50	40

and

$$EOL(A) = 85·5$$
$$EOL(B) = 76·5$$
$$EOL(C) = 3·5$$

The optimal action would be C and EOLI(I) = 3·5. This notation means 'the expected opportunity loss with the information of a forecast of outcome I'.

Outcome II forecast
Calculating the revised probabilities we obtain:

Outcome   *Probability*

I $\dfrac{0·10}{0·10 + 0·50 + 0·20} \times 0·20 = 0·025$

II   0·80   (forecast outcome)

III $\dfrac{0·50}{0.10 + 0·50 + 0·20} \times 0·20 = 0·125$

IV $\dfrac{0·20}{0·10 + 0·50 + 0·20} \times 0·20 = 0·050$

There is no need to repeat the COL table and we readily find

$$EOL(A) = 84·75$$
$$EOL(B) = 114·25$$
$$EOL(C) = 8·25$$

Again the optimal act is C and EOLI(II) = 8·25.

Outcome III forecast
The revised probabilities are:

Outcome   *Probability*

I $\dfrac{0·10}{0·10 + 0·20 + 0·20} \times 0·20 = 0·04$

II $\dfrac{0·20}{0·10 + 0·20 + 0·20} \times 0·20 = 0·08$

III   0·80   (forecast outcome)

IV $\dfrac{0·20}{0·10 + 0·20 + 0·20} \times 0·20 = 0·08$

Using this information

$$EOL(A) = 27·6$$
$$EOL(B) = 26·8$$
$$EOL(C) = 43·2$$

The optimal act is B and EOLI(III) = 26·8

Outcome IV forecast
Revising the probabilities we have:

Outcome   *Probability*

I $\dfrac{0·10}{0·10 + 0·20 + 0·50} \times 0·20 = 0·025$

II
$$\frac{0{\cdot}20}{0{\cdot}10+0{\cdot}20+0{\cdot}50} \times 0{\cdot}20 = 0{\cdot}05$$

III
$$\frac{0{\cdot}50}{0{\cdot}10+0{\cdot}20+0{\cdot}50} \times 0{\cdot}20 = 0{\cdot}125$$

IV
$$0{\cdot}80 \quad \text{(forecast outcome)}$$

This leads to

$$EOL(A) = 9{\cdot}75$$
$$EOL(B) = 144{\cdot}25$$
$$EOL(C) = 38{\cdot}25$$

The optimal act is A and EOLI(IV) = 9·75.

In practice, it was fairly obvious that the optimal acts would turn out as shown and then we need only have calculated the appropriate EOL for each forecast outcome. We present the full result for the sake of completeness.

We now complete the calculation by finding the overall EOLI from its four component parts. As we argued in the chapter we must use the original probability assessment in order to do this. We find

$$EOLI = 0{\cdot}10 \times EOLI(I) + 0{\cdot}20 \times EOLI(II) + 0{\cdot}50 \times EOLI(III)$$
$$+ 0{\cdot}20 \times EOLI(IV)$$
$$= 17{\cdot}35$$

The reader may wish to work the whole thing again using the other method of allocating the error to see how much difference it makes in this particular case.

Chapter 8 Decision-making with continuous probabilities

1. The best approach is to turn back a few pages and follow the method in the text. This starts by drawing a histogram, remembering that it is areas and not heights which matter in histograms. We therefore obtain Fig. S.1 in which the three rectangles are 0·3, 0·4, and 0·3 units of area respectively.

The three rectangles are now smoothed by drawing in a free-hand curve. This is, as we have said, a little subjective, though we shall check the end result against the original data. (We have adopted a slight short-cut in the method.)

Notice that the smooth curve starts at zero height for 0 loads/year but is not zero height at 30 000 loads/year. This follows from the Company's statement that the plant might be overloaded. Strictly, we should have a small 'tail' of the smooth curve extending to the right of 30 000 loads/year. In practice, there is no point in doing that because the Heath Robinson Engineering Company could not meet that part of the demand which was in excess of 30 000 loads/year. We therefore include the 'exceeds 30 000' part of the horizontal scale into the last class from 27 500 to 30 000. We can only do this because we were asked merely to smooth the curve for a 30 000 load plant, not to calculate how large a plant the Heath Robinson Engineering Company should build. Since we are now classifying all the demands in excess of 30 000 per year in the range 27 500–30 000 we still have to have the probabilities adding up to 1·00. This procedure may appear to be a little unsatisfactory but it does enable us to avoid having to make an assumption about the upper limit which the demand could reach.

The dotted lines in Fig. S.1 are now drawn to show the boundaries of the classes we are trying to create and, by counting the squares of graph paper under the smooth curve we find the proportion of area, and hence probability,—now lying in each of the new demand classes.

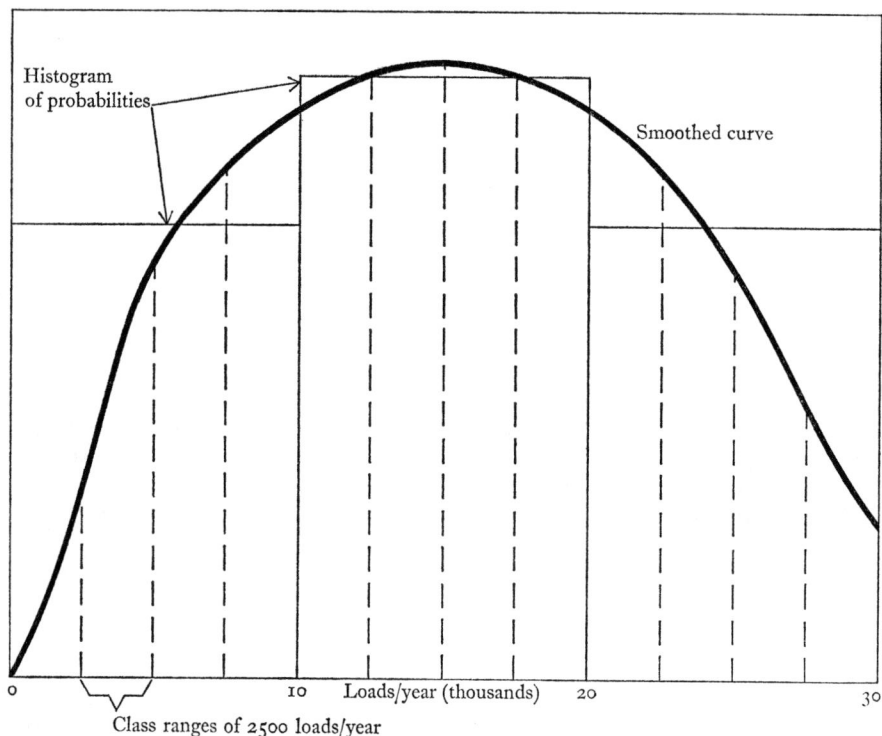

Fig. S.1 First stages in the solution

The results for Fig. S.1 are:

Demand range	Number of squares	Percentage of area, i.e., probability
0– 2500	21	1·8
2500– 5000	101	5·7
5000– 7500	156	8·8
7500–10000	195	10·9
10000–12500	200	11·2
12500–15000	203	11·3
15000–17500	200	11·2
17500–20000	191	10·6
20000–22500	175	9·7
22500–25000	150	8·4
25000–27500	110	6·2
27500–30000	75	4·2
	1777	100·0

The probabilities in the original ranges are now found by addition to be:

Range	Probability
0–10000	$1·8 + 5·7 + 8·8 + 10·9 = 27·2$
10000–20000	$11·2 + 11·3 + 11·2 + 10·6 = 44·3$
20000–30000	$9·7 + 8·4 + 6·2 + 4·2 = 28·5$

These three values are fairly near to the original ones of 0·3, 0·4, and 0·3. Counting squares is not a very accurate process, some rounding-off has been done to make the figures add to 100·0 and, in any case, the Heath Robinson Engineering Company's original figures were rather sweeping so there does not seem much point in refining the answer any further.

In a real case, however, it might well be thought advisable to make the two sets of values match more closely. To do this, one would redraw Fig. S.1 with the curve lowered between 10000 and 20000, or raised outside that range, re-count the squares and recalculate. It is only worth doing this about once because after that the tedium does not justify the improvement. After one revision of the curve it is easier simply to adjust the values in the probability column whilst keeping them proportioned much as they are. Drawing the free-hand curve the first time gives the right general shape and thereafter it is a matter of minor adjustment. The word 'right' in the last sentence is not used in the sense that 4 is the right answer to $2+2$. It is meant to imply that this is the general shape which most closely reflects the beliefs expressed in the probability statement embodied in the original histogram.

2. The loss function is very easily found. If the number of loads per year is L then the marginal profit will be £$10L$ at £10 per load and the loss function will be:

$$\text{Profit} = (L - 15\,000) \times 10$$

(It may seem odd to use the name 'loss function' for an equation from which one calculates profits. The terminology was really coined for problems like the one in the chapter and it has become standard.)

The calculation can be done in the following form:

Range	Mid-point (L)	Outcome (O)	Probability (P)%
0–2500	1250	− 137 500	1·8
2500–5000	3750	− 112 500	5·7
5000–7500	6250	− 87 500	8·8
7500–10 000	8750	− 62 500	10·9
10 000–12 500	11 250	− 37 500	11·2
12 500–15 000	13 750	− 12 500	11·3
15 000–17 500	16 250	12 500	11·1
17 500–20 000	18 750	37 500	10·6
20 000–22 500	21 250	62 500	9·7
22 500–25 000	23 750	87 500	8·4
25 000–27 500	26 250	112 500	6·2
27 500–30 000	28 750	137 500	4·2

The arithmetical labour can be reduced by noticing that the first half of the Outcome column is the negative of the second half. We therefore subtract the probabilities in the first half from those in the second half which correspond to the equal (but positive) outcomes. This gives

$$\begin{aligned}
\text{EV} = {}&12\,500 \times (0{\cdot}111 - 0{\cdot}113) + 37\,500 \times (0{\cdot}106 - 0{\cdot}112) \\
&+ 62\,500 \times (0{\cdot}097 - 0{\cdot}109) + 87\,500 \times (0{\cdot}084 - 0{\cdot}088) \\
&+ 112\,500 \times (0{\cdot}062 - 0{\cdot}057) + 137\,500 \times (0{\cdot}042 - 0{\cdot}018) \\
= {}&£2412
\end{aligned}$$

Utility theory might well have led to a different answer!

Notice, that with the original data and three-class breakdowns the expected value is exactly zero. Does the change from £0 EV to £2412 EV justify the steps taken in smoothing the data? Bear in mind that we adjusted the probabilities to take account of the Heath Robinson Engineering Company's belief that the demand might outrun the supply. This kind of question illustrates the two-fold nature of decision theory as a piece of mathematics and as an attempt to get inside the decision-making process. (See Chapter 9.)

3. We start by drawing the histogram, Fig. S.2, and then add the smoothed curve, taking account of the marketing directors views of the problem. The rather camel-shaped curve which appears is called a Bimodal distribution and is perfectly acceptable in statistical theory.

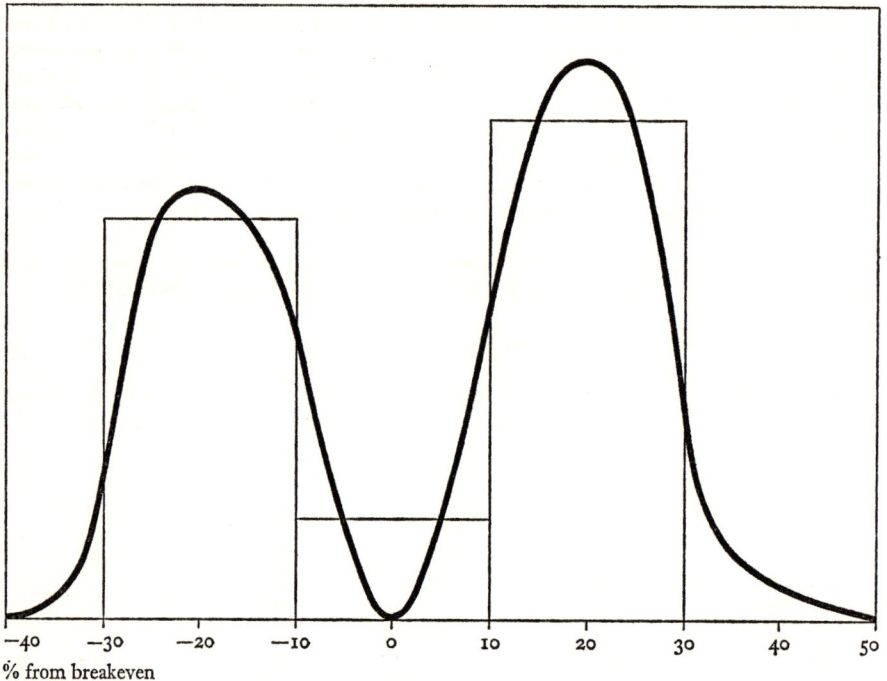

-40   -30   -20   -10   0   10   20   30   40   50

% from breakeven

Fig. S2 Solution of problem 3, Chapter 8

We now count squares for the new sub-ranges required by the smoothing and find:

Sub range		Units of area	Probability %
-40%	-30%	22	1·2
-30%	-20%	312	16·8
-20%	-10%	375	20·2
-10%	-0%	105	5·7
0%	10%	89	4·8
+10%	+20%	453	24·4
+20%	+30%	425	22·9
+30%	+40%	62	3·3
+40%	+50%	13	0·7
		1856	100·0

The probabilities for the original ranges, including the very small probabilities outside the original values, add up to

Original range	Original probability	New probability
-30% to -10%	40%	38·2%
-10% to +10%	10%	10·5%
+10% to +30%	50%	51·3%

4. The problem is solved by the following calculation

Demand range		Mid-point	Rate of pay off (mu/1%)	Amount of Pay off (mu)	Probability	EV
−40% to	−30%	−35%	−2	−70	0·012	−0·84
−30% to	−20%	−25%	−1·5	−37·5	0·168	−6·30
−20% to	−10%	−15%	−1	−15	0·202	−3·03
−10% to	0%	− 5%	−1	−5	0·057	−0·28
0% to	10%	5%	1·25	6·25	0·048	0·30
10% to	20%	15%	1·25	18·75	0·244	4·57
20% to	30%	25%	1·25	31·25	0·229	7·16
30% to	40%	35%	1·25	43·75	0·033	1·44
40% to	50%	45%	1·25	56·25	0·007	0·39
						3·41

The expected value for the project is 3·41 m.u.

Index